ASSESSMENT IN MIDDLE AND HIGH SCHOOL MATHEMATICS: A TEACHER'S GUIDE

Daniel J. Brahier

EYE ON EDUCATION
6 Depot Way West, Suite 106
Larchmont, N.Y. 10538

Library of Congress Cataloging-in-Publication Data

Brahier, Daniel J.
     Assessment in middle and high school mathematics : a teacher's guide / by Daniel J. Brahier.
          p. cm.
     ISBN 1-930556-20-9
      1. Mathematics--Study and teaching (Middle school)--Evaluation. 2. Mathematics--Study and teaching (Secondary)--Evaluation. 3. Mathematical ability--Testing. I. Title.

QA11 .B69988 2001
510'.71'2--dc21   2001023050

Production services provided by:
ComManagement
1211 Courtland Drive
Raleigh, NC 27604
(919)833-3350

Also Available from Eye On Education

A Collection of Performance Tasks And Rubrics:
High School Mathematics
By Charlotte Danielson and Elizabeth Marquez

A Collection of Performance Tasks and Rubrics:
Middle School Mathematics
By Charlotte Danielson

Bringing The NCTM Standards to Life:
Exemplary Practices From High Schools
By Yvelyne Germain-McCarthy

Bringing The NCTM Standards to Life:
Exemplary Practices For Middle Schools
By Yvelyne Germain-McCarthy

Open-Ended Questions in Elementary Mathematics:
Instruction and Assessment
By Mary Kay Dyer and Christine Moynihan

A Collection of Performance Tasks and Rubrics:
Primary School Mathematics
By Charlotte Danielson and Pia Hansen

A Collection of Performance Tasks And Rubrics:
Upper Elementary School Mathematics
By Charlotte Danielson

Mathematics The Write Way:
Activities For Every Elementary Classroom
By Marilyn S. Neil

Teaching Mathematics in the Block
By Susan Gilkey and Carla Hunt

INTRODUCTION

Following a long day of classroom teaching, I gathered up a set of test papers from my eighth grade mathematics class and took them home to grade them in the evening. After dinner, feeling exhausted from all of the work I had done that day, I pulled out the file of papers and a red pen. I decided that if I could get the "bad" papers out of the way, it would make the rest of my work much easier as I ran lower on energy. So, I began to sort the papers. I knew that Shannon was mathematically competent and would inevitably score an A on the test, so I put her paper on the bottom of the stack. Rachel had been struggling for weeks and participated very little in class, so I chose to score her test sooner, rather than later. Before I read the first paper, I already had them sequenced from what I anticipated would be the lowest to the highest grades.

Maybe I shouldn't have been surprised, but by the time I completed grading the tests that evening, I realized that my preconceptions of how students would perform were almost identical to their actual grades. And, like many other teachers, this wasn't the first time in my career that I was able to accurately predict student performance before looking at the tests. I couldn't help but ask myself, "If I already knew who my 'A' students were, which of my students were barely passing, and so forth, then why did I put them through the routine of taking a test and put myself through grading it in the first place?" Perhaps you have had the same experience and, if not, I recommend that you try pre-sequencing your tests like this some time. You, too, might be shocked at how much you already know about your students before reading the tests.

The reason why we know so much about our students is that we assess their progress in classes every day. Some of these assessments are more formal, such as looking over homework assignments or administering short quizzes; others are informal, such as observing student reactions to problems posed in class or asking an individual student a few interview questions when correcting an in-class assignment. More than 50 years ago, Sueltz, Boyton, and Sauble (1946) stated that "in general, observation, discussion, and interview serve better than paper-and-pencil tests in evaluating a pupil's ability to understand the principles and procedures he [sic] uses" (p. 145). So, the importance of getting to know our students by virtue of how they behave and interact in the classroom is not a new idea; instead, educators have come to rely on testing data as the ultimate measure of progress. While I am not ready to abandon traditional paper-and-pencil tests altogether, I will argue that if our assessment and grading processes do not include strategies such as classroom observations and student writing, we miss important windows into the thinking of our students. And if these strategies *are* being informally employed, perhaps a more standardized procedure of collecting the data would enhance our ability to assess student work and decrease our reliance on test scores. In short, if I already know who "gets it" and who doesn't, then giving the students yet another test may not be the best use of their class time. (Perhaps you have heard it said that one should not attempt to fatten a cow by weighing it more often!) Conversely, if students take a test, and the grades surprise me as their teacher — either students score much higher or considerably lower than I had anticipated — then perhaps I am the one who is in error. The test evidence would suggest that I have missed important cues in class that would have led me to a better understanding of my students' academic growth.

Several years ago, while teaching middle and secondary school mathematics, I began to realize the shortcomings of my assessment processes. Gradually, I phased in new strategies for collecting data on what my students could do and how they were thinking. I found myself using journals, open-ended questions, projects, and other techniques to supplement test data. I started to see my students in a different light and found that the better I got to know them as learners, the more prepared I felt to address their needs in the classroom. As a university mathematics educator, I conducted assessment inservice projects for teachers over a four-year span, assisting hundreds of other mathematics teachers in changing their classroom strategies and reflecting on their practice. This book, then, represents the culmination of efforts to reform my own teaching and to lead others in their professional development as well. The situations and examples described in this book are truly the work of practitioners — "real life" scenarios and suggestions that have been field-tested and shown to be effective in my own work.

As a university mathematics educator, I also continue to teach an eighth grade mathematics class every day to test my ideas and keep in touch with the school setting. I have served as a principal, guidance counselor, and curriculum director in my career as well, and these roles have helped me to view the role of assessment in a number of different ways. For example, when a parent challenges the grade issued by a teacher to a high school student, the first question often asked is, "What kind of data did you collect on which to base these grades?" As an administrator, I quickly learned about the importance of gathering specific, ongoing information about each student's performance for settling disagreements as well as adding credibility to discussions at parent-teacher conferences. The teacher who could pull out a binder and show a parent a sample of the student's work was much more helpful than the teacher who could do little more than tell the parent that "Anne has a 67% average in my class."

Assessment in Middle and High School Mathematics: A Teacher's Guide is organized into five chapters, sequenced in the same order that the assessment projects for teachers, discussed previously, were conducted for four years:

CHAPTER 1: WHY CHANGE ASSESSMENT PRACTICES?

The opening chapter provides a rationale for why a teacher might want or need to change classroom assessment strategies in the first place. This chapter includes a discussion of student work and a rationale for change as recommended by the National Council of Teachers of Mathematics in the Standards documents.

CHAPTER 2: ALTERNATIVES FOR ASSESSMENT

Four different alternatives for teachers to consider in changing their assessment practices are described in this chapter — open-ended questions and rubrics, journals, projects and presentations, and observations. While there are many non-traditional alternatives available for educators to consider in reforming their practices, my work with teachers who are interested in improving their classroom assessment has shown these to be the most practical and attainable "first steps." Later, teachers may want to explore other assessment strategies, such as the use of formal interviews and portfolios of student work.

CHAPTER 3: SAMPLE ASSESSMENTS

After having described the various assessment alternatives in Chapter 2, this chapter turns to looking at specific examples of *how to* use these four strategies in one's daily teaching practice. The ideas presented in this chapter are concrete, practical, and field-tested. They are designed to be directly implemented by teachers as a means of "getting their feet wet" in making changes, as well as to serve as models that can be adapted to local needs. Ideas are presented that illustrate a variety of content topics at several skill and grade levels.

CHAPTER 4: DETERMINING FINAL GRADES

This chapter deals with another very practical question that frequently arises in teacher inservice presentations: How do I use all of this data that I've collected to arrive at a final grade for students in my classes? The question is realistic and pivotal as one considers the implementation of various assessment alternatives. The chapter looks at the various purposes for assessment, as suggested by the National Council of Teachers of Mathematics in the Standards documents. Examples illustrate the variety of ways in which assessments can be used. Some of the assessments are useful in determining grades, while others are helpful for information gathering but may not affect a student's grade at all.

CHAPTER 5: TAKING THE FIRST STEP

The last thing a teacher wants to do is to get excited about making a change but commit to such an elaborate shift in classroom practices that the result is "doing nothing" because "I can't change everything." Sternberg, Torff, and Grigorenko (1998) wrote that one of the major reasons why teachers resist reform is that "teachers often don't know how to implement the theories in the classroom, and they recognize (correctly) that incorrect implementations of a theory can do more harm than good" (p. 667). This chapter sets the reader up for success and describes some practical ideas for implementing assessment practices in "baby steps" or incremental stages over time and developing specific assessment plans to assist with the change. The strength of these assessment plans can be measured against the assessment Standards benchmarks established by the NCTM, which are also described in this chapter.

APPENDIX: OTHER AVAILABLE ASSESSMENT RESOURCE MATERIALS

Finally, the Appendix of this book lists or describes over 130 books, journal articles, Web sites, and videos that illustrate or describe various assessment alternatives, providing additional examples and ideas for teachers who are rethinking their assessment practices.

The intent of this book is to be practical and helpful to the inservice or preservice teacher who is considering the use of a variety of non-traditional assessment practices in the classroom. I hope that it motivates change and leads you to a greater appreciation for the role of assessment in mathematics, while setting the stage for additional changes you may choose to make in your work as a teacher of mathematics.

ACKNOWLEDGMENTS

The publication of a book like this certainly doesn't happen by itself. I would like to thank my family — my wife, Anne, and my three sons, John, Mark, and Luke — for their patience and understanding throughout the long hours of researching, writing, and revising the manuscript. I would also like to thank Daniel Joyce for reading the text as it was developed and providing immediate and valuable feedback from the perspective of a veteran mathematics teacher. A special thanks goes to Heather Moore for her countless hours of searching Web sites and identifying resources for the book, including the Appendix. I want to express my appreciation to Michael Crane, Durfee High School, Fall River, Massachusetts and Wendy Sanchez, University of Georgia for their thoughtful reviews of the manuscript's first draft and to Bob Sickles at Eye On Education for getting this project off the ground.

I would like to acknowledge the Assessment Project teaching staff at Bowling Green State University — Sarah Carver, Janet Emerine, Deb Gallagher, Laura Little, and Bill Speer — as well as the hundreds of participants from ASPECT, ASPEN, ASPIRE, and ASCEND, for their ideas and risk taking in the endeavor of changing assessment practices. I am also grateful to the Ohio Board of Regents' Eisenhower Program, without whose funding these programs would not have been possible, and to Russell Utgard and Pei-Hsing Wu for their support of the assessment projects. Finally, thanks goes out to my students at St. Rose School in Perrysburg and my middle and secondary school mathematics methods classes at Bowling Green State University for allowing me to field test ideas and gather their input.

REFERENCES

National Council of Teachers of Mathematics. (1995). *Assessment Standards for School Mathematics*. Reston, VA: NCTM.

Sternberg, R.J., Torff, B., & Grigorenko, E. (1998). Teaching for successful intelligence raises school achievement. *Phi Delta Kappan*, 79 (9), 667-671.

Sueltz, B.A., Boynton, H., & Sauble, I. (1946). The measurement of understanding in elementary-school mathematics. In *The Measurement of Understanding*, 45th Yearbook of the National Society for the Study of Education, Pt. 1. Chicago: University of Chicago Press.

TABLE OF CONTENTS

ABOUT THE AUTHOR

Daniel Brahier is an Associate Professor of Mathematics Education at Bowling Green State University, where he has served since 1994. He earned his Ph.D. from the University of Toledo in Curriculum and Instruction, with a major in Mathematics Education and a minor in Educational Administration. Throughout his career, Dr. Brahier has taught secondary and middle school Mathematics and Earth Science, and served as a Principal, Guidance Counselor, and District Curriculum Consultant. He teaches one section of Eighth Grade Mathematics at St. Rose School in Perrysburg, Ohio, which he has been doing since 1989.

At Bowling Green State University, Dr. Brahier teaches Secondary, Middle Childhood, and Early Childhood undergraduate mathematics and mathematics methods courses, as well as graduate courses in mathematics education, curriculum, and assessment. He is the Mathematics Education Advisor for all students at BGSU who major in Secondary Integrated Mathematics Education. He was the Project Director of a four-year Eisenhower-funded Assessment Project which served 225 teachers from 12 counties in Northwest Ohio between 1995 and 1999. He directed a Discrete Mathematics Institute with funding from the National Science Foundation at BGSU in 1995 and 1996 and is currently conducting two study groups of elementary school teachers involving four school districts in Northwest Ohio (Projects SUCCESS and SUCCESS II) with funding from the Ohio Board of Regents' Eisenhower Program. He has conducted hundreds of workshops throughout the United States and has made presentations in Mexico and Australia.

Dr. Brahier's first book, *Teaching Secondary and Middle School Mathematics* and its accompanying Instructor's Manual, were released by Allyn & Bacon Publishers in November of 1999. The textbook is designed for undergraduate and graduate courses preparing secondary or middle school teachers. Dr. Brahier serves on the Editorial Panel for the Mathematics Teaching in the Middle School for the National Council of Teachers of Mathematics and has authored four World's Largest Math Event documents for NCTM since 1997.

1

WHY CHANGE ASSESSMENT PRACTICES?

"The way I assess my students' performance in mathematics already seems to be working, so why should I change?"

Suppose that you had just completed teaching a mathematics unit on determining compound interest. You want to know whether your students grasped the effect of interest compounding over time. You might consider one or some combination of the following assessments:

♦ Give the students a written test with 10-20 compound interest questions such as: *If $2,500 is invested at 8% interest, compounded annually, how much interest will it earn in 10 years?*

♦ Give the students a written test with 5-10 compound interest problems such as: *Suppose that you invest $5,000 in the bank for 15 years. If, at the end of that time, you have a total of $10,000 in your account, determine the approximate average annual interest rate that your money has earned.*

♦ Give the students two days to complete a short project with the following directions: *Suppose that you want to put $1,000 in the bank on the first day of each year from now until you retire at age 65. Examine the effects of earning an average of 5% interest per year versus 7% interest per year. How much more interest will you earn between now and retirement if you can average 7% rather than 5% annual interest?* (Interestingly, over the course of 50 years, the 7% average rate will yield over $200,000 more in interest — nearly double the amount of money — than the 5% rate!)

All three of these assessment scenarios will allow you to collect data about your students' ability to determine compound interest. So, how do you go about deciding which assessment is most appropriate for your class? Certainly, there are several factors that are likely to drive your decision. First, the assessment should reflect the intent of the objectives stated in the course of study. Teachers in School District A may have a course of study that states, "Given the principal, time period, and the annual interest rate, the student will be able to determine the amount of compound interest for an investment." On the other hand, School District B's curriculum may read more broadly, such as, "The student will be able to explain the effects of compound interest and determine interest over a given period of time." The first objective is very specific and skill-oriented, whereas the second outcome emphasizes conceptual understanding of compound interest. Therefore, a teacher from School District A may elect to use a straightforward, 20-question test, while a teacher in District B may feel the need to use richer problems or even projects to determine whether a student has met the stated outcome. On the other hand, there is no rule that precludes a teacher in District A from using a project to assess student progress, but it is probably unrealistic for a teacher in District B to attempt to measure the conceptual outcome with a 20-question, skill-based written test.

Another factor that often motivates a teacher's decision on how to assess students is whether the teacher has emphasized skill development, conceptual understanding, or application of a mathematical process in classroom activities. It would be unfair, for example, to ask a class of students who spent four days working traditional interest problems on worksheets to demonstrate their understanding by conducting a complex project. The evaluation Standards of the National Council of Teachers of Mathematics (NCTM) describe the notion of *alignment* by stating that "the degree to which meaningful inferences can be drawn from . . . an assessment depends on the degree to which the assessment methods and tasks are aligned or are in agreement with the curriculum" (NCTM, 1989, p. 193). A stated curriculum and a teacher who emphasize conceptual development and application of a skill *should* assess students by using a more complex task to adequately measure success.

A high school teacher, writing for *Mathematics Teacher* journal and struggling with the inconsistencies between her teaching and assessment, asked the reader to "look at the most recent test that you gave to your class. How many questions asked students to investigate? Were students asked to formulate? Did they need to apply a variety of strategies? How many questions asked students to repeat memorized algorithms to solve isolated problems?" Reflecting on the changes she had made in her classroom teaching routines, she noted that, "I realized that although my instruction had shifted toward NCTM's vision, my assessment practices had not" (Murphy, 1999, p. 248). So, it is important that the assessment tasks given to our students be consistent with the way that the class was taught the mathematical content in the first place — assessment needs to mirror instruction.

Finally, teachers select assessment tasks based on their own beliefs about the use for mathematics and their understanding of the content they are teaching (see, for example, Cooney, Badger, & Wilson, 1993). So, if you value skill development and believe that the ability to compute compound interest is the cornerstone of this area of the curriculum, then this belief will drive your teaching and, ultimately, your assessment strategies. However, if you believe that application of a skill is necessary to demonstrate understanding, then you may opt to ask higher-level test questions or assign a project in your assessment of student progress.

The purpose of this book, then, is not necessarily to change your views about the nature of mathematics because you probably already think of the discipline as more than the memorization of rote procedures, or you would not be reading the suggestions provided here. At the same time, you might find it helpful to reflect on the assessments that you have tried in the past. Think about whether it was the wording of the curriculum, the need for consistency between instruction and assessment, your beliefs about and knowledge of the content, or some combination of these factors that generally drive your decisions. Then, ask yourself, "What would my classroom look like if I used more of the complex tasks and projects for assessment?" And, more importantly, "How would the students in my class develop differently if I changed the focus of my instruction and my assessment to an emphasis on higher-level thinking and processing skills?" The latter question is extremely important, as researchers such as Cuban (1993) have determined that teachers will only change if they can be persuaded that doing business differently will benefit both themselves and their students.

Let's explore some examples of how different types of assessments can be used to demonstrate a variety of levels of student thinking. These are actual assessments from middle and secondary classrooms that have been compiled over time.

EXAMPLES OF STUDENT ASSESSMENTS

SQUARE ROOT OF A NUMBER

In a large school district with 30,000 students in the Midwest, children were given a competency test in the eighth grade year to assess their understanding of key concepts in the district's course of study. The objective under study was one that read, "The student will be able to determine a square root and explain its meaning." For five years, the district assessed this outcome by asking four multiple-choice items, such as:

Find the square root of the number:

$\sqrt{25}$ A.   4
        B.   5
        C.   6
        D.   7

To demonstrate mastery of this outcome, a student had to answer three of the four questions correctly, *and* they were allowed to use a calculator. After discovering that students had shown 100% mastery of this objective for five years in a row, a central office administrator asked, "Do we really know if the students *understand* the concept of square roots, or can they simply compute its value properly with a calculator?" The following year, the question was changed to the following:

What number has a square root of approximately 13.42? Explain how you know.

To answer this item accurately, of course, the student had to recognize that if , then $\sqrt{x} \approx 13.42$ could be found by determining that $(13.42)^2 \approx 180$. A calculator alone does not help a student to answer this question correctly, unless the student can use it as a tool and knows to square 13.42. In the next two years of the competency testing program, only 17% of the eighth graders answered this question correctly! Therefore, there were many students who could effectively use a calculator to determine a square root but who had little, if any, understanding of the concept of "square root." And, of course, this revelation about the level at which students understood square roots did not arise until the question — the assessment item — was asked in a different way that emphasized conceptual understanding over computational ability.

SOLVING PROPORTIONS

In an Algebra 2 course made up primarily of high school sophomores, students had been working with proportions, including setting them up to model problems and finding their solutions. The teacher asked the students two questions on a simple assessment:

1. Solve: $\dfrac{24}{x} = \dfrac{3}{2}$

2. Explain how you know that your answer is correct.

Not surprisingly, every student in the class was able to solve the simple proportion given in question #1 to find that $x = 16$. However, only a couple of students were able to adequately justify their correct answers. The answers to question #2 varied, but many students responded with a mechanical, algorithmic statement such as:

The correct answer is x=16. Multiply the top number of the first proportion by the lower number of the 2nd proportion. This is called "cross-multiplying." Then divide that answer by 3, the last number there is that has not been used to figure out "x."

An examination of this response shows a lack of conceptual understanding for what it means for a proportion to be true. Instead, the response is a mechanical description of "how to do it." Also, the student misuses the term *proportion* by referring to each fraction in the equation as a separate proportion. Another student responded with the following answer:

x = 16 because I changed them around until I got the right answer because 3 is higher than 2 and there can't be 3 parts of 2

According to this response, the student inverted the fractions in some way to find the missing value, but it's not clear exactly how the problem was solved. Note that the question of how the student knows that the answer is correct is never addressed and that the student carries a misconception that "there can't be 3 parts of 2." However, the student apparently believes that it is possible to have 2 parts of 3.

Both of these responses are significant because asking a student to solve a proportion and provide a missing number does not get to the heart of the student's understanding of *proportion* on a conceptual level. In both cases, the students found the correct value for *x* but were unable to explain how they knew it was correct. Furthermore, the responses revealed misconceptions that would not have surfaced if only question #1 had been asked.

COMPUTATION AND NUMBER SENSE

Principles and Standards for School Mathematics (NCTM, 2000) emphasizes that, in addition to learning how to perform computation with numbers, educators should recognize the importance of developing number sense — "the ability to decompose

numbers naturally, use particular numbers like 100 or $\frac{1}{2}$ as referents, use the relation-

ships among arithmetic operations to make sense of numbers, and recognize the relative and absolute magnitude of numbers" (p. 32). Of course, the way that we assess student understanding of numbers and operations will influence our beliefs about what they can and cannot do.

A study by Reys and Yang (1998), for example, showed that children at the sixth and eighth grade levels were far more proficient in their ability to do computation with fractions than to answer questions regarding fraction concepts. For example, when

students were asked to compute $\frac{12}{13} + \frac{7}{8}$, 61% of sixth and 63% of eighth graders were

able successfully to find the sum. (You can ask yourself whether these percentages are acceptable for the grade levels and why eighth graders did not perform significantly better than sixth graders, despite two more years of "practice.") However, when students were given a multiple-choice question to determine the best estimate for the same sum and given the choices of 1, 2, 19, 21, and "I don't know," only 25% of the sixth and 38% of the eighth graders were able to select the correct choice. While 61% of sixth graders could do the computation question by hand, 65% of them selected 19, 21, or "I don't know" when asked for a reasonable estimate to the very same question later in the test. The question, of course, required nothing more than recognizing that each addend is approximately equal to 1, so the sum would be about 2. Similarly,

when students were asked whether $\frac{3}{8}$ or $\frac{7}{13}$ was closer to the value of $\frac{1}{2}$, only 10% of

the sixth and 28% of the eighth graders were able to answer correctly and provide a reasonable explanation. In general, these middle school students were able to do paper-and-pencil computation but were found to possess little number sense.

In another recent research study conducted with children in grades one through five, Clark and Kamii (1996) showed how students often conduct multiplication computation without an understanding of the operation. The authors stated that "multiplicative thinking appears early (among 45% of second graders) and develops very slowly. A surprising finding is that only 49% of the fifth graders are solid multiplicative thinkers" (p. 48). They concluded that teachers should not expect all students to be able to properly use multiplication, even as late as the fifth grade. This study, of course, runs counter to popular opinion that students should "learn," "memorize," and even take timed tests on multiplication facts in the third and fourth grade. It may well be that students have the facts memorized but do not understand the process of multiplication at all. Their study, incidentally, mirrored research by O'Brien and Casey (1983) in which children were asked to create a story problem that involves 6 x 13, and almost half of the fifth graders generated problems like "There are six ducks swimming in the pond. Then a while later three more ducks come, so how many are there?" (p. 248). Again, the theme is that students are often able to compute with numbers but lack a sense of the size of numbers, the meaning of the operation, or the reasonableness of the answer. But we only find this out if we *ask* students to demonstrate something beyond simple computation.

In our final example of number sense, a curriculum coordinator for a large urban district observed a group of fourth graders taking a five-question quiz on rounding to the nearest 10. Students were asked to do the following:

Round each number to the nearest 10:

1.   27   _____
2.   13   _____
3.   89   _____
4.   45   _____
5.   21   _____

Sara responded by putting answers of 30, 20, 90, 50, and 21 on the answer blanks. The teacher "graded" the paper and scored her responses as "3 out of 5 correct," recorded it in the grade book, and told the curriculum coordinator that the paper indicated Sara was on her way to understanding rounding but probably needed more practice. After the class period, the coordinator briefly interviewed the student and asked her to explain her thinking. She responded, "Well, the teacher told us to look at the number in the one's place and the number next to it. If it's bigger, you round up, and if it isn't, you leave it alone. The '3' is bigger than the '1', so it should be rounded up just like the '7' is bigger than the '2'. But since the '1' is smaller than the '2' in 21, you're supposed to leave that number alone, aren't you?" Clearly, Sara had missed the point at which the teacher said "greater *than five*" and assumed she was supposed to compare the relative magnitudes of the digits in the number.

This brief interview showed that the issue was not "needing more practice" at all. Instead, Sara never understood the concept of rounding in the first place and had improperly memorized a rule. The teacher could have simply asked one question on the quiz: "Round 23 to the nearest 10 and explain how you got your answer." This single question would reveal the thought process of each child, providing not only a set of scores but an insightful look into the window of student thinking in the classroom. But without a required written explanation or some type of interview, the teacher is left to speculate on the reasons for a student's errors and may not be able to properly assist the class. In general, the results of traditional testing methods that rely primarily on computation exercises where answers are written on "blanks" will not reveal the misconceptions possessed by our students and are, therefore, not of much use when designing curriculum or modifying instruction.

STANDARDIZED TESTING

Fortunately, many of the standardized tests that are currently being administered to students in mathematics have begun to include items that provide evidence of conceptual understanding, rather than (or in addition to) the student's ability to answer direct, simplistic questions. The results of these assessments, then, can be rich in terms of the evidence they provide to assist educators in making instructional decisions. Consider, for example, the 1996 National Assessment of Educational Progress (The Nation's Report Card). The following question was posed to high school seniors on the test:

> Luis mixed 6 ounces of cherry syrup with 53 ounces of water to make a cherry-flavored drink. Martin mixed 5 ounces of the same cherry syrup with 42 ounces of water. Who made the drink with the stronger cherry flavor? Give mathematical evidence to justify your answer. (Reese, et al., 1997, p. 22)

The problem involves a simple comparison of the values of two fractions. However, notice that twelfth graders were not simply asked to change a given fraction to a decimal or to place an inequality symbol in a mathematical sentence. Instead, they had to problem solve by using their skills and justifying their responses. Furthermore, the item was scored on a 3-point rubric or grading scale. For a student's response to be considered "satisfactory," the student had to identify Martin as having the stronger drink and provide a reasonable mathematical explanation. On the 1996 NAEP exam, only 23% of high school seniors were able to provide a satisfactory response. As we saw with the examples on computation and number sense, students are often able to perform a basic skill, such as changing a fraction to a decimal, but are unable to use the skill in the context of solving a simple word problem like this one.

On the High School Proficiency Test in New Jersey (1992), eleventh grade students were asked four open-ended or free-response questions, in addition to 36 multiple-choice items. One of the questions was as follows:

Use the table and information below to answer [the question]. The table indicates the hourly receipts for Farrah's Fast Food on a typical day.

6-7 a.m.	$65	12-1 p.m.	$320	6-7 p.m.	$305
7-8 a.m.	$105	1-2 p.m.	$240	7-8 p.m.	$200
8-9 a.m.	$230	2-3 p.m.	$150	8-9 p.m.	$170
9-10 a.m.	$190	3-4 p.m.	$125	9-10 p.m.	$110
10-11 a.m.	$110	4-5 p.m.	$150	10-11 p.m.	$70
11–12 a.m.	$195	5-6 p.m.	$220	11-12 p.m.	$45

Farrah's is open from 6 a.m. to 12 midnight; a manager is always present. Farrah, the owner, has 8 counterpersons working for her every day during the hours Farrah's is open. Each counterperson works 7 consecutive hours sometime during the day. Typically, each counterperson takes in up to $80 per hour while working.

Based only on the information in this problem, develop a master schedule for 8 counterpersons for a typical day. Ignore any breaks taken by the counterpersons. The master schedule should satisfy the following conditions:

1. The schedule indicates the 7-hour block of time during which each counterperson is working.

2. There are always enough counterpersons working to handle the typical volume of business.

3. There will be times when more counterpersons are working than are needed. However, those times are minimized.

Clearly, this question calls upon students to reason mathematically and to solve a problem couched in a very real-life setting. The purpose for the free-response item is to place high school juniors in a decision-making situation and assess their ability to analyze the scenario and communicate a response that makes sense. The authors of the examination are communicating to the students and to the taxpayers that simple paper-and-pencil skills are not sufficient to be successful in a technologically-dominated world. We continue to see the inclusion of these types of items on local, state, and national assessments as an outgrowth of the recommendations made by the National Council of Teachers of Mathematics (NCTM) in the Standards documents. In the next section, an overview of the Standards and their implications will be provided.

THE ASSESSMENT STANDARDS

In 1995, after two years of refining and gaining the input of thousands of educators who read the initial draft, NCTM released the document entitled *Assessment Standards for School Mathematics.* In the assessment Standards, the authors define assessment as "the process of gathering evidence about a student's knowledge of, ability to use, and disposition toward, mathematics and of making inferences from that evidence for a variety of purposes" (NCTM, 1995, p. 3). We need to recognize that *any* collection of data in the classroom — formal or informal — that informs our practice is considered assessment. So, while testing is one form of assessment or data gathering, so is observing the students and noticing who is paying attention, who is taking notes, who is volunteering answers, and who is slouching in a chair. The cumulative effect of assessing students is to provide the teacher with a clear picture of how students are developing their understanding of and attitudes toward the mathematical content and processes.

The Standards also remind us that the assessment process is ongoing, passing through four phases that are inherently linked to one another: (a) Planning Assessment, (b) Gathering Evidence, (c) Interpreting the Evidence, and (d) Using the Results. The authors note that "the phases . . . should not be seen as necessarily sequential" and that "assessment does not proceed through [the phases] in a neat, linear fashion" (NCTM, 1995, p. 4). Figure 1.1 illustrates the connection between these stages.

FIGURE 1.1. THE FOUR PHASES OF ASSESSMENT

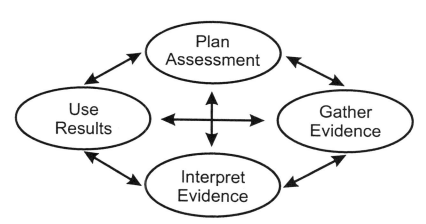

(NCTM, 1995. Reprinted with permission.)

So, as teachers, we are constantly in the process of planning for, implementing, reflecting on, and using our assessments. The authors of the Standards also identify a number of questions that relate to each phase of the assessment process that can be useful for reflecting on one's practices. The questions are as follows:

DECISIONS OCCURRING WITHIN EACH ASSESSMENT PHASE

Planning the assessment

♦ What purpose does the assessment serve?

♦ What framework is used to give focus and balance to the activities?

♦ What methods are used for gathering and interpreting evidence?

♦ What criteria are used for judging performances on activities?

♦ What formats are used for summarizing judgments and reporting results?

Gathering evidence

♦ How are activities and tasks created or selected?

♦ How are procedures selected for engaging students in the activities?

♦ How are methods for creating and preserving evidence of the performances to be judged?

Interpreting the evidence

♦ How is the quality of the evidence determined?

♦ How is an understanding of the performances to be inferred from the evidence?

♦ What specific criteria are applied to judge the performances?

♦ Have the criteria been applied appropriately?

♦ How will the judgments be summarized as results?

Using the results

♦ How will the results be reported?

♦ How should inferences from the results be made?

♦ What action will be taken based on the inferences?

♦ How can it be ensured that these results will be incorporated in subsequent instruction and assessment?

(NCTM, 1995, pp. 4-5. Reprinted with permission.)

Historically, many educators have equated "assessment" with "evaluation" or "giving grades." But the contemporary definition of assessment and some reflection on these four phases serve to broaden the process to mean more than evaluating a student's performance. Instead, we challenge ourselves to use assessment data to drive decisions that we make in the classroom, to validate our teaching or the local curriculum, and in a general sense, to tailor our classroom environment to the needs of our students. No one will deny that it is necessary in most institutions to "give grades," and the use of appropriate assessment strategies will enable teachers to do that. (For a detailed discussion on determining grades, refer to Chapter 4.) However, if the intent is to help our students achieve as well as possible, then it is crucial that we also use our assessment data to get to know them better, personally and mathematically. The discussion of the "Ideal Line of Inference" in the next section will further illustrate the importance of broadening our thinking about assessment.

THE IDEAL LINE OF INFERENCE

At some point in one's educational career, almost every student has the experience of "bombing" a test, even though the student was confident, had studied hard, and was ready to take the exam. Conversely, most students have also walked into a test with apprehension and a great deal of stress but managed to "ace" the test anyway, seemingly due to the choice of questions on the exam or the luck of the student to select or guess correct answers. How often have we heard our students say, "I really knew this stuff. I didn't miss any homework problems all week, and I studied hard, but I still got a 'D' on the test!"

Of course, from the teacher's side of the desk, the experience is equally frustrating. We have a student who generally sleeps in class and rarely does homework but can routinely pull A's and B's on our tests. Likewise, we have students who come to school early for extra help, have a tutor, and do every homework assignment but experience some form of test anxiety that keeps them from scoring any higher than a C on our tests. Somehow, we would like to see the former student being assigned a grade lower than an A or B and the latter student maintaining a grade higher than a C — a grade that they truly deserve — but our tests do not tell the whole story. Intuitively, we know that the numbers fall short of the big picture, but we struggle to gather relevant data that support our image of these students. In short, we want our assessments and grades of our students to accurately reflect their classroom performances.

A model referred to as the Ideal Line of Inference (Brahier, 1997) can be used to demonstrate how assessment occurs in the classroom. Figure 1.2 illustrates this model in which we acknowledge that academic achievement progresses on a continuum, where some students have no understanding of a concept, while others demonstrate partial understanding, and others attain complete comprehension. (This, of course, is different from traditional thinking about student achievement in mathematics. Instead of viewing the acquisition of mathematical knowledge as "having it" or "not having it,"

FIGURE 1.2. THE IDEAL LINE OF INFERENCE MODEL

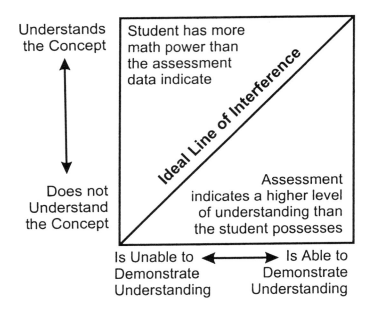

the model recognizes the continual development of mathematical ideas. Over the course of time, students move upward on the vertical axis as they develop their conceptual understanding.) Likewise, some students can demonstrate their level of understanding fairly well on an assessment, while others have considerably more difficulty, due in part to the student's discomfort with the assessment strategy being employed. As a result, teachers attempt to conduct classroom assessment practices in a way that student evaluations will fall on the Ideal Line of Inference, a line that indicates a "perfect" match between what the student knows and what the assessment process measures. However, even teachers with little classroom experience are keenly aware that many students fall under this line: They are able to "fake" their way through a test, for example, but really do not understand the concepts. This often occurs because the test does not accurately match the intended outcomes, as we saw earlier in this chapter with our discussion of the square root assessments. On the other hand, some students really do understand the concepts at hand but experience difficulty in taking a written test and are, therefore, unable to demonstrate their level of comprehension. As a result, they fall above the Ideal Line of Inference because, again, the assessment tool falls short of measuring the wide range of abilities of the student.

Experience with professional development activities shows that many inservice teachers believe their students fall fairly close to the Ideal Line of Inference until they actually try to administer alternative assessments. Then, they quickly discover that some of the students who were earning the highest grades have significant gaps in their understanding. Similarly, some of their lower achievers demonstrate considerably clearer understanding of concepts when given the opportunity to write about a problem or to explain it in an interview. The aim, then, becomes devising an assessment program for your students that is the most successful at placing them on the Ideal Line of Inference — an assessment plan that will allow you comfortably and confidently to report student achievement. The process of actually developing such an overall assessment plan is described in detail in Chapter 5.

As you may realize by now, written tests alone do not generally act as an accurate tool with which to infer student achievement. So, we turn to other assessment strategies — "authentic" or "alternative" ideas — to supplement our test scores and place our students' achievement more closely to the Ideal Line of Inference. There are many alternatives to traditional testing and quizzing, including the use of free-response questions scored on a rubric, journals, interviews, projects, presentations, observations, checklists, and portfolios. Any one or combination of these alternatives, together with more traditional tests, quizzes, and homework assignments, can significantly enhance your ability to measure student achievement and to tailor your classroom to student needs. The process of change and improvement, then, begins with an exploration of several alternatives that are available to the classroom teacher and a consideration of the strengths and potential drawbacks of each technique, which will be pursued in Chapter 2.

CONCLUSION

Have you ever had a picture taken of yourself, only to look at it later and say, "That's not really 'me'!"? In fact, if someone routinely snaps one picture of you, depending on the day of the week, on how you had your hair combed, and so forth, the photograph may or may not portray what you want to display on someone else's fireplace mantle as "you." It always helps to have an additional picture or two — one, perhaps, from the side, and one in which you are posed differently or wearing different clothes. After all, why do you think a professional photographer takes numerous photographs of you or your family with a variety of backgrounds and poses and then asks you to go through them to pick your favorite? If someone views a set of photographs of you in different clothes and from different angles, you might feel comfortable that, as a group, the pictures truly illustrate what you look like. Given a variety of pictures, you might even feel comfortable with selecting one or two of them and claiming that they best represent you.

In a similar way, our students are often tested on a regular basis, and those test scores — given on one particular day and containing one set of teacher-selected questions — are used to tell the entire story of their academic progress. We sometimes hear students proclaim that "if I would have been able to show you what I mean and explain it to you, I think you would agree that I understood it. The test just didn't show what I really know." And perhaps they are onto something. Maybe if we had assessed them through some informal interviews, by writing journals, or some other alternative strategies and then combined these data with test, quiz, and homework information that we had already collected, we could have assembled a more holistic view of the student that transcends the score on a paper-and-pencil examination.

In this chapter, we have explored the general issue of student assessment in mathematics. We illustrated the shortcomings of tests that serve as lone assessors of student progress and discussed the importance of assessment aligning with curriculum and instructional practices. Viewing assessment through the lens of the NCTM assessment Standards, we looked at assessment as an ongoing process of data collection over time that is used not only to evaluate students but to provide feedback that helps us adjust and refine our teaching practices. Finally, we looked at the notion of the Ideal Line of Inference and how the use of a variety of assessment tools can be used to gain a clearer picture of student progress.

Changing one's assessment strategies does not necessarily mean that a teacher has to work *harder*; instead, it means that a teacher can work *smarter* — a phrase often used in the business industry. In other words, implementation of assessment alternatives does not have to result in additional work being *added to* the teacher's responsibility. Instead, it can *replace* some of what teachers already do and enhance teaching performance in the classroom. Most teachers who attempt to use new and different forms of assessment very quickly begin to realize the benefits of this practice. There are a variety of authentic assessments that teachers can use, but this book will focus primarily on four of them — open-ended questions scored on rubrics, journals, projects and presentations, and observations. We will limit ourselves to these four strategies because the author's experience with staff development projects conducted with teachers has shown these to be the most realistic and widely-attempted approaches used by middle and high school mathematics teachers. In the next chapter, we explore each of these four strategies and the way they can be effective tools to measure student progress if they are used in your classroom.

REFERENCES

Brahier, D.J. (1997). Using assessment practices as a tool for changing teaching methodology. In J.A. Dossey, J.O. Swafford, M. Parmantie, & Anne E. Dossey (Eds.), *Proceedings of the Nineteenth Annual Meeting of the North American Chapter of the International Group for the Psychology of Mathematics Education*, 115-121. Columbus, OH: ERIC Clearinghouse for Science, Mathematics, and Environmental Education.

Clark, F.B., & Kamii, C. (1996). Identification of multiplicative thinking in children in grades 1-5. *Journal for Research in Mathematics Education, 27* (1), 41-51.

Cooney, T.J., Badger, E., & Wilson, M.R. (1993). Assessment, understanding mathematics, and distinguishing visions from mirages. In N.L. Webb (Ed.), *Assessment in the mathematics classroom: 1993 Yearbook of the NCTM*, pp. 239-247. Reston, VA: NCTM.

Cuban, L. (1993). *How teachers taught: Constancy and change in American classrooms 1880-1990* (2nd ed.). New York: Teachers College Press.

Murphy, T. (1999). Changing assessment practices in an algebra class, or "will this be on the test?" *Mathematics Teacher*, 92 (3), 247-249.

National Council of Teachers of Mathematics. (2000). *Principles and Standards for School Mathematics*. Reston, VA: NCTM.

National Council of Teachers of Mathematics. (1995). *Assessment Standards for School Mathematics*. Reston, VA: NCTM.

National Council of Teachers of Mathematics. (1989). *Curriculum and evaluation Standards for School Mathematics*. Reston, VA: NCTM.

New Jersey Department of Education. (1992). *Eleventh grade high school proficiency test*. Trenton, NJ: New Jersey DOE.

O'Brien, T., & Casey, S. (1983). Children learning multiplication. *School Science and Mathematics*, 83, 246-251.

Reese, C.M., Miller, K.E., Mazzeo, J., & Dossey, J.A. (1997). *NAEP 1996 Mathematics Report Card for the Nation and the States*. Washington, DC: National Center for Education Statistics.

Reys, R.E., & Yang, D-C. (1998). Computation and number sense among students in Taiwan. *Journal for Research in Mathematics Education*, 29 (2), 225-237.

2

ALTERNATIVES FOR ASSESSMENT

"Is this going to be on the test?"

How often have we heard this familiar question in our daily teaching? Each time that a teacher begins a lesson, gives an assignment, or asks students to take out their notebooks, there is bound to be someone in the class who asks this question. So, what does this query mean? In the eyes of a teenager, it translates to the following: "Is this important? Because if it's on the test, I'll know that you think it's important and pay close attention. But if you never intend to test me on it, then it'll never affect my grade. So, there's really no need to know it, and I can spend the time dreaming about my first car instead." Indeed, this famous question is at the heart of assessment because, as the authors of the NCTM assessment Standards state, "Students have learned that what is assessed and how it is assessed reflect what educators value" (NCTM, 1995, pp. 4-5). If we think about classes that we have taken in our educational career, we can all think of instructors who placed a high value on tests and others who placed more significance on projects or written papers. The college-level instructor who relies on two tests — a midterm and a final exam — to comprise an entire grade in a class sends the message to the students that only content knowledge is valued, not their ability to write papers, give presentations, or even attend class. Conversely, if we are members of a class in which grades rely on interviews, posting our thinking to a class listserve, or doing long-term individual and group projects, in addition to or in place of tests, the structure of the class again tells us what the instructor values.

Take a minute to think about your own classroom and how you assess (or plan to assess) student progress. If someone were to interview your mathematics students and ask them what *you* believe is important in your class, how are they likely to respond? A logical guess might be that they will express what you value based on the way that you determine their grades. If, for example, you collect their class notes and grade them for accuracy and completeness, the students in your class are likely to say that you value "note taking." If you grade tests solely on whether solutions to problems are correct or incorrect, students will say that you believe that "right answers" are important but that you don't necessarily value their thinking processes.

17

There are two high school teachers who work across the hall from one another in a school on the West Coast. Ms. Taylor collects homework every day and "grades" each question as right or wrong, assigning a percentage correct to each student as a homework score. Mr. Deacon also collects the assignments every day but assigns credit to the students based on whether they attempted every problem on the homework, regardless of whether solutions are correct. Which of these methods do you prefer? What do we learn about Ms. Taylor and Mr. Deacon's values by virtue of the way they count homework grades? And, more directly, the question is: What are *your* students learning about the nature of mathematics in light of the assessments that *you* use? Are you sending out the "right" messages? In the larger picture, are you confident that the assessments you use are adequately determining student progress while providing you with feedback that helps you to teach more effectively?

In Chapter 1, we discussed the importance of using a variety of assessment strategies to appropriately capture the total range of student achievement in the classroom. Supplementing traditional tests with other assessment strategies can be a useful method of getting our assessments to more closely match what we referred to as the Ideal Line of Inference. At the same time, these other assessments can be helpful in getting students to recognize that we, as teachers, value more than correct answers — we value the process of *doing* mathematics as well. In *Principles and Standards for School Mathematics* (2000), the National Council of Teachers of Mathematics (NCTM) describes five mathematical processes: Problem Solving, Reasoning and Proof, Communication, Connections, and Representation. As students develop their content knowledge, the authors of the Standards note, they should also be learning to think, reason, and "do" mathematics. If we agree that mathematical thinking is an important component of the classroom, then it makes sense that our assessments would attempt to measure this thinking, which goes well beyond "getting right answers" on a written test or homework assignment.

There are many alternatives available to teachers of mathematics for assessing their students. Instead of relying entirely on written tests, several techniques have become widely used since the advent of the Standards documents, as these assessments tend to provide a more authentic view of a student's capabilities. In the remainder of this chapter, we will explore four strategies: (a) open-ended questions and the use of rubrics, (b) journal writing, (c) projects and presentations, and (d) observations. We will focus on the *how* each of these strategies can be employed in the classroom, along with some advantages and possible drawbacks to each. Specific activities and ideas for each of these assessment methods are detailed further in Chapter 3.

OPEN-ENDED QUESTIONS AND RUBRICS

Whether in a classroom or not, there are generally two types of questions that one can ask: a *closed* question (one that has one, direct answer) and an *open-ended* question (one that elicits a variety of responses). For example, if a student is asked, "What is the least common denominator for the fractions $\frac{2}{3}, \frac{3}{4}$, and $\frac{1}{8}$?" we are expecting a student to respond with "24" — a single, expected, correct answer. On the other hand, students could be asked to "write a letter to a friend, explaining how one determines the least common denominator for the fractions $\frac{2}{3}, \frac{3}{4}$, and $\frac{1}{8}$." In the latter case, there are several ways that a student may explain the process, including anything from making a list of multiples of 3, 4, and 8 until the first "match" is identified, to laying out a line of Cuisenaire rods of lengths 3, 4, and 8, until the segments are the same length, to factoring the denominators using a "tree" and multiplying the "different" prime factors.

Clearly, the open-ended question has the potential to more accurately assess student thinking processes than the closed version of the question. Of course, the closed question is very easy to score — the student either got the correct answer or did not. The open-ended question demands a more careful assessment since there are a variety of ways to answer the question and not just one correct answer.

Consequently, many teachers have turned to using a grading scale called a *rubric* on which to score student responses. The rubric is simply a set of guidelines or benchmarks that measure student success on a performance item such as an open-ended question, presentation, project, or similar assessment. The teacher's task, then, is to determine the level at which the student responded. Many states and national testing companies are using open-ended questions on standardized tests and scoring papers on rubrics. The following 4-point rubric is an example of a scoring scale and is used to assess open-ended items on Ohio's proficiency tests:

MATHEMATICS SCORING RUBRIC FOR EXTENDED RESPONSE QUESTIONS

Extended—response items are scored on a 4-point scale using the following criteria:

4

♦ Contains an effective solution

♦ Shows complete understanding of the concept or task

♦ Addresses thoroughly the points relevant to the solution

♦ Contains logical reasoning and valid conclusions

♦ Communicates effectively and clearly through writing and/or diagrams

♦ Includes adequate and correct computations and/or setup when required

(A four-point response may go beyond the requirements of the item.)

3

♦ Contains minor flaws

♦ Indicates an understanding of the concept or item

♦ Communicates adequately through writing and/or diagrams

♦ Generally reaches reasonable conclusions

♦ Contains minor flaws in reasoning and/or computation, or neglects to address some aspect of the problem

2

♦ Indicates gaps in understanding and/or execution

♦ Contains some combination of the following flaws:

An incomplete understanding of the concept or item

Failure to address some points relevant to the solution

Faulty reasoning

Weak conclusions

Unclear communication in writing and/or diagrams

A poor understanding of relevant mathematical procedures or concepts

---

1

♦ Indicates some effort beyond restating the item or copying given data

♦ Contains some combination of the following flaws:

Little understanding of the concept or item

Failure to address most aspects of the item or solution

Major flaws in reasoning that led to invalid conclusions

A definite lack of understanding of relevant mathematical procedures or concepts

Omission of significant parts of the item and solution or response

---

0

♦ Indicates no mathematical understanding of the concept or item

---

Ohio Department of Education (2000).

Notice that each level, from bottom to top, represents an increasingly higher level of sophistication in the response. Instead of measuring student answers against other students — which happens all too often across the content areas in education — the rubric serves as an objective set of criteria that represents the expectations for a "good" answer. The rubric can also be individualized for a particular open-ended item or any performance task assigned to students. Samples of rubrics that can be used for journal entries and projects are presented in some detail in the next chapter. Teachers interested in using open-ended questions (sometimes referred to as "free-response" questions) often begin by having students respond in writing to one or two of these questions per week, either for practice or in the form of a quiz. Open-ended questions can also be incorporated into more formal, written unit tests. There are several advantages and drawbacks to using open-ended questions in the mathematics classroom.

ADVANTAGES TO USING OPEN-ENDED QUESTIONS AND RUBRICS

♦ The use of open-ended questions promotes mathematical communication and reasoning. As students work to express their thinking in words and with diagrams, the five mathematical processes are developed.

♦ Responses to open-ended questions provide a useful window into student thinking. Teachers can more accurately identify misconceptions and tailor future lessons accordingly.

♦ Open-ended questions send out a message to students about the nature of mathematics. Students "learn" that more than correct answers are valued in the classroom and that mathematics often transcends "right" and "wrong" answers or approaches.

POSSIBLE DRAWBACKS TO USING OPEN-ENDED QUESTIONS AND RUBRICS

♦ Students who are not accustomed to responding to mathematical questions with sentences and/or drawings often resist open-ended questions. They may have been conditioned to believe that all problems in mathematics classes can be answered with a number or word written on a line.

♦ More time is often spent grading open-ended questions on a rubric than it takes to check "right" and "wrong" responses written on answer blanks. Once teachers have practiced using open-ended questions, their scoring methods become more efficient, and this concern generally disappears. But, at first, the time commitment can be a major stumbling block for teachers making a change.

♦ Open-ended questions may not align with instructional techniques or a district's testing program. If students, for example, are not frequently asked these types of questions in the classroom, it may be unrealistic to expect them to respond to an open-ended question on a more formal assessment.

The use of open-ended questions can be a very powerful way to collect data about student performance, but both teachers and students need to develop a comfort level for using this type of assessment. Interestingly, rubrics have been used in other content areas for decades. In fact, probably the best authority on using a rubric in a building is the English (Language Arts) teacher who uses such a scale to grade essays and term papers. However, since the strategy is relatively "new" to mathematics, it takes time for the teacher and the students to develop a comfort level for asking and assessing open-ended questions. Another common strategy for assessing student progress that is also no stranger to the English or Social Studies teacher is the use of a journal.

JOURNALS

Journals have been widely used in classrooms other than mathematics for many years. Typically, teachers require students to have two spiral notebooks — one for taking daily notes and one for writing journal entries. Then, students are given regular opportunities to write in their journals. While some teachers find it useful to have students write in the journal every day, others have students write two to three entries per week. To a large degree, the frequency of journal entry writing depends on the number of students taught by the teacher. If a high school teacher has six classes with 25 students in each class, it is probably not realistic to ask students to journal every day because the teacher is not likely to have the time to read all of the entries. On the other hand, the lines of communication between a student and the teacher are greatly enhanced with frequent writing in a journal, so it is important to provide students with regular writing opportunities.

At the beginning of the school year, a teacher can provide students with very specific *prompts* — questions or statements that provide the basis on which a student can generate a journal entry. For example, a teacher may ask the students questions such as:

♦ How are the lines $y = -\dfrac{1}{2}x + 5$ and $y = 2x - 7$ related to one another? Explain how you know.

♦ If two dice are rolled, are you more likely to roll a 6, a 7, or an 8? Or, are the probabilities the same? Explain.

♦ What is the effect on a cosine curve's graph when the function has a negative coefficient (e.g., the difference between the graphs of $y = 2\cos x + 3$ and $y = -2\cos x + 3$)? Draw a picture to show what you mean.

As the school year progresses, however, journal prompts can become more "open," allowing for students to take the entries in a direction of their own choosing. For example, prompts a teacher might provide later in the school year might include the following:

♦ What was the most difficult topic we studied this week? What made it difficult for you?

♦ Choose a homework problem with which you had difficulty last night, explain why it was difficult, and explain how to solve it properly.

♦ Complete this thought in a paragraph or two: In this class, I wish we would spend more time . . . because . . . , but I am glad that we . . . because . . .

As students become more comfortable with writing in a journal, they will be able to deal more effectively with open-ended prompts such as these. Teachers generally collect journals every couple of weeks and read student responses. Sometimes, written comments made back to the student are appropriate, and other times, the teacher chooses to simply read the entries and indicate that the journal has been read. For example, one junior high school girl wrote in her journal:

I'm glad that we keep journals in our math class. A lot of times you ask us to explain how to do a certain kind of problem. I don't know how to do it or explain it when I start my journal entry, but by the time I finish my writing it has forced me to go back over the concept and I actually understand it. The journal makes me review what we do in class and think about it before the next day.

In turn, the teacher wrote back to the student and told her that he was impressed with how she was able to make sense of the lesson each day as she wrote her entry. The journal conversation became an excellent way of establishing communication between the teacher and an otherwise introverted student.

Journal entries may be non-graded, or they may be scored on a rubric, which will be described in more detail in Chapter 3. Many teachers who have been using very traditional means of assessment throughout their careers find journal writing a comfortable entry into alternative assessments. Some advantages and possible drawbacks to using journals in the classroom are as follows:

ADVANTAGES TO USING JOURNALS

♦ Journals allow students to not only *solve* mathematical problems but to *reflect* on their problem-solving processes. When asked to describe how they solved a problem or how they reacted to a topic presented in class, students are challenged to engage in metacognition — the process of analyzing their own thought processes ("thinking about how they think").

♦ Journals provide an ongoing means of communication between individual students and the teacher. Often, students will write a question or concern in a journal that they would not necessarily raise in the classroom, allowing the teacher to address an issue that has not surfaced in class.

♦ Journals work hand-in-hand with open-ended questions because they provide opportunities for students to practice writing about how they solved problems. Journal writing can help students to respond more effectively to open-ended questions.

POSSIBLE DRAWBACKS TO USING JOURNALS

♦ As is the case with open-ended questions, students who are not used to writing in a mathematics class will often resist journal writing because it is a non-traditional approach to learning mathematics. They also may be annoyed by the fact that two or more of their teachers are requiring journals. Therefore, a middle or high school teacher is wise to ask other teachers if they use journals in their classes so that students are not overwhelmed and receive a consistent message about the role of journaling in all of their classes.

♦ Generating meaningful prompts and keeping up with the reading of journals can be very time-consuming for the teacher. As is the case with any change in practice, a teacher will eventually develop a list of effective prompts and ways to efficiently review journals, but getting used to the inclusion of journals in the assessment process can be time-intensive.

♦ Organizing the journals themselves can be a confusing task. If students take the journals home to write entries, the notebooks can be lost during the school year. But if journals are kept in the classroom on a shelf, the teacher has to provide the opportunity for doing all writing during class time. Also, when journals are collected, they are not as easy physically to take home to grade as a stack of papers. Imagine routinely taking home a stack of 150 notebooks!

Many middle and high school teachers collect journals on a rotating basis. For example, they might collect First Period's journals on Tuesday, Second Period's on Thursday, and Third Period's the following Wednesday. Teachers in self-contained upper-elementary or middle school classrooms often code the journals with colored sticky dots and collect "red dots" on Monday, "yellow dots" on Wednesday, and "blue dots" on Friday. Using these types of strategies, the teacher does not have to try to read an overwhelming number of journals in a given night or over a weekend. As is the case with any new assessment strategy, it is important for the teacher to think carefully about how most effectively to assimilate the technique into a pre-existing routine. However, the use of journals can prove to be very worthwhile. And the time spent in reading them can lead to hours of time saved later when the teacher often realizes too late that students have formed major misconceptions and that re-teaching is necessary. Another important strategy for assessment in a Standards-based classroom is the use of student projects and presentations. This technique will be discussed in the next section.

PROJECTS/PRESENTATIONS

A middle school mathematics class, engaged in a unit on data analysis, was concerned that the intersection located near the school was over-congested. Local residents had requested that a traffic light be installed, but officials were not convinced that the crossroads were busy enough to warrant a new light. So, as a mathematics project, students took shifts and sat at the street corner to gather data on the number of cars passing through the intersection at given time periods over the course of two weeks. Then, each team of three or four students made a presentation to the class in which they described their findings and made a recommendation on installing a traffic light. Eventually, the class submitted their findings to the City Council to influence its decision on the matter.

In a Pre-calculus class, students had been exploring the graphs of trigonometric functions. Pairs of students were asked to select a city, use the Internet to access the average high and low temperatures over the course of a year, and fit a sine curve on the scatterplot of the data to generalize the changes over time and make predictions about the future. Each pair of students selected a different city and then submitted its results in the form of a written paper the following week.

These two scenarios are examples of how a teacher can use team or individual projects and presentations to assess student progress in the areas of data analysis and trignonometric functions without necessarily giving a traditional "test" in these areas. Both of the projects place the students in realistic situations, as the middle school students try to make a case for a new traffic light near the school, while high school students use a sine curve to predict future temperatures for the city of their choice. The project represents a more long-term approach to assessment, rather than giving students 45 minutes to solve a set of paper-and-pencil problems.

The popularity of projects is on the increase, as teachers have begun to recognize that projects not only provide important assessment data on student understanding, but also tend to be motivating to many students due to the "real life" nature of the problems. The TIMSS-R report (Third International Mathematics and Science Study — Repeat) shows that middle school students in the United States report solving "real life" problems in their mathematics classes more often than the international average (Gonzales et al., 2000). However, the report also shows that while 59% of eighth graders in the United State report that they conduct science projects as part of their classes "almost always" or "pretty often," only 29% of those students reported doing projects in their mathematics classes. Instead, the typical U.S. mathematics classroom is still dominated by doing worksheets or problems from textbooks, with 86% of the students reporting that class time is primarily comprised of this activity. Clearly, there is much to be done in the area of implementing projects and presentations in mathematics, even though we recognize the many benefits of this assessment strategy. The following are some advantages and drawbacks to using projects and presentations:

ADVANTAGES TO USING PROJECTS/PRESENTATIONS

♦ The assessment can be a learning experience, as students come to an appreciation for the application of mathematics in solving real-life problems.

♦ Project assessments allow students to do their work over time and to make corrections and revisions before turning in a final paper or making a presentation. When a student takes a traditional test, there is generally no opportunity after the test day to go back and rethink or revise any of the problem solutions.

♦ Projects can allow for the assessment of students' ability to integrate and connect mathematical ideas. The project may be rooted in data analysis, for example, but also require students to represent information in a variety of ways, to make predictions, and to communicate mathematical ideas to others by oral or written means.

POSSIBLE DRAWBACKS TO USING PROJECTS/PRESENTATIONS

♦ Since projects are often completed in small groups, the teacher has to decide how to assess student work individually when it is submitted in the context of a group assignment. (Specific suggestions for this will be described in the next chapter.)

♦ Every class is different, as are local courses of study, so it can be difficult to design effective projects for students. Ideas presented in resource books may or may not apply to a teacher's classroom; therefore, project ideas often have to be modified to "fit" a specific situation. Some creativity and a commitment of time may be necessary for a teacher to effectively research and implement projects and class presentations.

♦ Teachers need to decide whether the information collected from a project is sufficient to determine student progress for a particular unit and whether a more traditional assessment is also needed. If students make class presentations, these discussions can also use valuable class time, which the teacher must weigh against other ways to use the time.

Projects and presentations can be most effectively assessed by using a stated set of criteria (rubric) for scoring them. The rubric can be particularly effective when the students themselves are asked to construct the criteria that could be used to measure their work. If students are involved in the development of the rubric, they take ownership in the idea and are more likely to have a clear understanding of expectations for the project. As students work on projects in class, teachers have an excellent opportunity to observe them. Observations and the use of checklists will be the final strategy discussed in this chapter.

OBSERVATIONS

Teachers routinely observe the actions of their students in the classroom every day. From watching a group of students interact on a collaborative project to observing the facial expressions of individuals during a presentation, formal and informal monitoring of student reactions is a regular occurrence in the life of a teacher. However, few take the time to structure observations and collect data in a meaningful way so that instructional decisions can be derived from the observations. The NCTM (1989) stated that "information is best collected through informal observation of students as they participate in class discussions, attempt to solve problems, and work on various assignments individually or in groups" (p. 233). If we believe that observational data can be powerful in assessing student progress, then some standard procedures and strategies are needed.

While students were solving a complex problem, one teacher walked around the room with a sheet of mailing labels, writing down the student's name, the date, and observational notes on each label. After class, the teacher peeled off the labels and stuck them to individual sheets bearing the names of students in the class, which were three-hole punched and inserted in a binder of student records. Over time, the teacher collected numerous observational notes about the behavior of each student that could be shared at parent-teacher conferences. Similarly, another teacher used post-it notes on which to write observational comments and stuck them on the students' desks while walking around the room. This method provided students with immediate feedback on how they were behaving, and the teacher collected them at the end of class to re-stick them in a binder of observational data. Neither of these data collection methods required any more work than the teacher would have done anyway, and there was no copying of information to be done after class. The teachers merely created a procedure for structuring the collection and analysis of observational data for future reference.

Similarly, some teachers have designed or adapted checklists of expected student behaviors. During class work, they circulate about the classroom, "checking off" the observed activities as a way of keeping track of on-task classwork. In some cases, they have developed simple rubrics such as "2 = Always," "1 = Sometimes," and "0 = Never," as a code for recording behaviors on an established checklist. They even involve their students in defining the behaviors that advance mathematical discourse so that students take an active role in the development of the checklist itself. Examples of checklists and how to design them are detailed in the next chapter. Some advantages and potential drawbacks to using observations are as follows:

ADVANTAGES TO USING OBSERVATIONS

- ◆ Observational data represent "real time" and allow the teacher to record what is seen during class time. Whereas test results provide "end-of-the-chapter" information, observational data document ongoing, formative information that can be helpful in restructuring a lesson or unit.

- At parent-teacher conferences, meetings with student services personnel such as guidance counselors or administrators, or in phone call correspondences with parents, observational data can be helpful in succinctly describing how the student behaves during class time.

- Observation does not add to the workload of a teacher. Teachers routinely watch students while they work anyway, so the use of observations and checklists simply formalizes the process, providing concrete data that can have an impact on the teaching and learning process.

POSSIBLE DRAWBACKS TO USING OBSERVATIONS

- An observational note is merely a "snapshot" of a student at a particular time, as we discussed in Chapter 1. Students have been heard to lament that "you didn't see me when I was *really* contributing to the group's work," which can be a very realistic flaw in conducting observations (though not very different from a student claiming after a test that "you didn't ask questions about the things I studied the most!"). Teachers need to take these data in context, placed alongside of other assessment information in order to obtain the total picture of student performance.

- Recording open-ended observational notes can be time-consuming. While making a note about one student's behavior, the teacher might miss significant actions of others in the class. And, while the construction of checklists can alleviate this problem during class time, the process of devising a checklist can also be difficult and time-intensive.

- Parents and students may have difficulty with the use of observational data for determining final grades, since they view the collection of these data as "subjective" and, therefore, biased. Discussions on the use of observational data in determining grades will be included in both Chapters 3 and 4.

There is much to be learned about student progress and the effectiveness of a lesson simply by watching the way students behave. A raised hand and a smile tells us as much as a head on the desk and a lack of participation. As teachers, the feedback we obtain during class can be considerably more useful than test or quiz scores. And, as we use observation and checklists to gather information, students learn that their behavior during class time is valued and will, in fact, affect their grades. Consequently, the observation assessment strategy can also promote effective classroom management and discipline as students know that their behavior "counts." There is probably no more powerful method of assessing student progress than systematically observing students as they work in class. The key, of course, is to make the process *systematic*.

CONCLUSION

Perhaps you have heard it said that "nobody can change everything, but everyone can change something." The purpose of this chapter is not to suggest that all teachers

FIGURE 2.1. SUMMARY OF ADVANTAGES AND DISADVANTAGES OF ASSESSMENT ALTERNATIVES

STRATEGY	ADVANTAGES	DISADVANTAGES
Open-ended questions and the use of rubrics	◆ The use of open-ended questions promotes mathematical communication and reasoning. ◆ Responses to open-ended questions provide a useful window into student thinking. ◆ Open-ended questions send out a message to students about the nature of mathematics.	◆ Students who are not accustomed to responding to mathematical questions with sentences and/or drawings often resist open-ended questions. ◆ More time is often spent grading open-ended questions on a rubric than it takes to check "right" and "wrong" responses written on answer blanks. ◆ Open-ended questions may not align with instructional techniques or a district's testing program.
Journals	◆ Journals can allow students to not only *solve* mathematical problems but to *reflect* on their problem-solving processes. ◆ Journals provide an ongoing means of communication between individual students and the teacher. ◆ Journals work hand-in-hand with open-ended questions because they provide opportunities for students to practice writing about how they solved problems. Journal writing can help students to more effectively respond to open-ended questions.	◆ As is the case with open-ended questions, students who are not used to writing in a mathematics class will often resist journal writing because it is a nontraditional approach to learning mathematics. ◆ Generating meaningful prompts and keeping up with the reading of journals can be very time-consuming for the teacher. ◆ Organizing the journals themselves can be a confusing task. If students take the journals home to write entries, the notebooks can be lost during the school year. But if journals are kept in the classroom on a shelf, the teacher has to provide the opportunity for doing all writing during class time.

Projects and presentations	◆ The assessment can be a learning experience, as students come to an appreciation for the use of mathematics in solving real-life problems. ◆ Project assessments allow students to do their work over time and to make corrections and revisions before turning in a final paper or making a presentation. ◆ Projects can allow for the assessment of students' ability to integrate and connect mathematical ideas.	◆ Since projects are often completed in small groups, the teacher has to decide how to assess student work individually when it is submitted in the context of a group assignment. ◆ Every class is different, as are local courses of study, so it can be difficult to design effective projects for students. Ideas presented in resource books may or may not apply to a teacher's classroom. ◆ Teachers need to decide whether the information collected from a project is sufficient to determine student progress for a particular unit and whether a more traditional assessment is also needed.
Observations	◆ Observational data represent "real time" and allow the teacher to record what is seen during class time. ◆ At parent-teacher conferences or in phone call correspondences with parents, observational data can be helpful in succinctly describing how the student behaves during class time. ◆ Observation does not add to the workload of a teacher. Teachers routinely watch students while they work anyway, so the use of observations and checklists simply formalizes the process.	◆ An observational note is merely a "snapshot" of a student at a particular time. Teachers need to take these data in context. ◆ Recording open-ended observational notes can be time-consuming. And, while the use of checklists can alleviate this problem during class time, the process of devising a checklist can also be difficult and time-intensive. ◆ Parents and students may have difficulty with the use of observational data for determining final grades, since they view the collection of these data as "subjective" and, therefore, biased.

should be utilizing all four of these assessment strategies, along with their more traditional testing and homework procedures from the past. In fact, simply *adding* some of these strategies to what they already do (or plan to do) probably is not a good idea. Instead, the four assessment alternatives described in this chapter — open-ended questions and rubrics, journals, projects and presentations, and observations — are intended as a sampler of possibilities for teachers seeking change in their assessment systems. Figure 2.1 summarizes the advantages and possible drawbacks of each method described in this chapter:

One person, for example, may already be using journals but has never really thought about systematically collecting observational data. Another teacher may be using projects but has not tried having students respond to open-ended questions with regularity. It may not be possible — or even desirable — to adopt *all* of the strategies briefly outlined in this chapter. Instead, each individual needs to consider the strategies that are already being used and ask, "Which, if any, of these techniques might enhance my ability to assess student progress?" Any one or combination of the strategies discussed in this chapter may help to build a more effective assessment program. The logistics of deciding what to change and how to change will be discussed in some depth in Chapter 5.

At this point, you may be acknowledging your need to update your assessment practices but be unsure which "new" strategy to employ. Or, you might have decided on a new course of action but are looking for more specific ideas. The purpose of Chapter 3 is to present examples of each of the four strategies described here. The examples are not intended to be comprehensive, but will help to provide a picture of the type of possibilities that are available as teachers consider the use of open-ended questions, journals, projects, and observations. Specific activities, rubrics, and checklists will be provided, serving as models and ideas from which to begin to structure change in your classroom. In addition, the Appendix includes over 130 other resources for specific classroom ideas, including books, journal articles, Web sites, and videos.

REFERENCES

Gonzales, P., Calsyn, C., Jocelyn, L., Mak, K., Kastberg, D., Arafeh, S., Williams, T., & Tsen, W. (2000). *Pursuing excellence: Comparisons of international eighth-grade mathematics and science achievement from a U.S. perspective, 1995 and 1999.* Washington, DC: National Center for Education Statistics.

National Council of Teachers of Mathematics. (2000). *Principles and standards for school mathematics.* Reston, VA: NCTM.

National Council of Teachers of Mathematics. (1995). *Assessment standards for school mathematics.* Reston, VA: NCTM.

National Council of Teachers of Mathematics. (1989). *Curriculum and evaluation standards for school mathematics.* Reston, VA: NCTM.

Ohio Department of Education. ODE Web site. WWW document [www.ode.state.oh.us]. (accessed 2/01)

3

SAMPLE ASSESSMENTS

"But how can I actually make this work in my own classroom?"

Getting started with any new idea in the classroom can be the most difficult step. Once you have "gotten your feet wet" with an alternative assessment strategy, one thing can lead to another until you are conducting business much differently within a few months than you were at the beginning of a school year. One of the most common questions raised by participants at teacher workshops is, "I like the idea of using journals (or open-ended questions, interviews, and so forth), but I can't picture what it would look like in *my* classroom. I need more specifics to help me get started." Indeed, if the first two chapters of this book got you thinking about your classroom assessment practices, and you have decided that you would like to try something new, you may be looking for some more detailed explanations and examples of the four methods addressed in Chapter 2.

The purpose of this chapter is to provide you with additional assistance. Practical explanations on how to use each of the four strategies will be presented, along with some sample assessments to get you started. Obviously, between the differences in grade levels and classes taught by the readers and the variety in local courses of study, these examples will not be able to do "everything" for "everyone." You may be able to use some of these suggested assessments "as is" and modify others for use in your own classroom. But even if they are only used as models and further examples, the ideas suggested in this chapter should set the tone for change in your classroom. Armed with some detailed explanations and examples, you can begin to research other sources cited in the Appendix, take a second look at your teachers' manuals, and talk to colleagues as you begin to broaden your approach to assessment. We will begin by looking at how to write and score open-ended questions.

SAMPLE OPEN-ENDED QUESTIONS AND RUBRICS

Open-ended (sometimes referred to as "free-response" or "extended-response") questions are intended to elicit a variety of solutions. These questions fall into two categories, which need to be considered when writing, asking, or scoring an item. In the first case, the item has a specific "correct" answer but a variety of ways of getting to the answer. The second type of open-ended question does not necessarily have only one acceptable response.

Consider the diagram in Figure 3.1. The student has been asked to find the area of the shaded region.

FIGURE 3.1. FIND THE AREA OF THE SHADED REGION

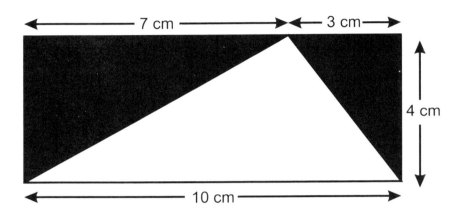

In this case, the shaded region's area is 20 square centimeters. But there are at least three different ways that the student may have arrived at this answer, including the following:

- Find the area of the rectangle $(10 \times 4 = 40)$ and subtract the area of the "unshaded" triangle inside $(\frac{1}{2} \times 10 \times 4 = 20)$ to find the area of the remaining, shaded region.

- Find the area of each of the two shaded triangles $(\frac{1}{2} \times 7 \times 4 = 14$ and $\frac{1}{2} \times 3 \times 4 = 6)$ and add them together to find the total area of the shaded region.

- Recognize that if the smaller shaded triangle were slid over and connected to the larger shaded triangle, the shape would be the same as the unshaded triangle. Therefore, the area of the shaded region must be exactly one-half of the area of the rectangle, so its area would have to be $\frac{1}{2} \times 10 \times 4 = 20$.

There is only one "correct" answer in this case: 20 sq. cm. But there are multiple ways of arriving at this solution. The teacher, therefore, is more concerned with student thinking and how the problem was approached than simply knowing if the student could arrive at 20 sq. cm. as the answer. Recall from Chapter 1 that this type of question emphasizes to the student that we are interested in the problem solving and reasoning exhibited in the item and not simply in the correct answer. As such, the problem itself (and the way that it is assessed) sends out a message to the student about the nature of mathematics and what the teacher values.

Anytime that a teacher asks students to "show all of your work" or "explain how you found your answer" but anticipates a particular solution with several potential approaches, we have an open-ended question of this first type. Taking it a step further, suppose that one wants to score student responses to this question on a rubric or standardized grading scale. A simple 3-point rubric could be designed, as follows:

---

3 *(Excellent Response)*

The student finds the correct answer of 20 sq. cm. and demonstrates, through a drawing or with words, a thorough understanding of how to find the area of a rectangle and/or triangle.

2 *(Acceptable Response)*

The student finds the correct answer of 20 sq. cm., but the explanation or drawing accompanying the solution is sketchy. The student has not clearly communicated the method by which the answer was determined. OR, the student may have a correct and elegant explanation for how to find the correct answer but arrived at a solution other than 20 sq. cm. (a computational error results in a "wrong" answer).

1 *(Partial Response)*

The student attempts to explain a method for finding the area, but the method has an error (for example, the student might have used an incorrect formula for finding area of a triangle). An error in method leads to an incorrect answer, so the student has not found the solution to be 20 sq. cm. either.

0 *(No Response)*

The student left the item blank or wrote down something that appears to be nothing more than copying down the given information or diagram.

Some educators disagree philosophically with the way this rubric is written, claiming that "if students have the right answer, why should they be penalized for not providing an accurate explanation?" Consequently, they will argue that as long as a student found the correct answer of 20 sq. cm., that student deserves to receive a "3" on the item. (Note that a correct answer without a clear explanation currently earns the student a "2" on the scale.) Notice that the reverse is also true: The student can earn a "2" without finding the correct answer, as long as a reasonable game plan for determining the solution has been described. The answer to this concern, of course, goes back to what we value in the classroom. If we want our students to know that it's not good enough to just find answers and that we value mathematical reasoning and communication, then this rubric — as stated — serves the purpose. The rubric a teacher designs for an open-ended item, a homework assignment, a project, and so forth, should purposefully illustrate what is important and valued in that classroom. Individual teachers may or may not agree with the philosophy of the rubric presented here, but it is intended to "put teeth" into the argument that students should be able to communicate mathematically. Remember that students will rise to the teacher's expectations if they are told that it will "be on the test" and that the way they respond will affect their grade.

We also often hear educators ask, "So, what is the difference between scoring a paper on a rubric and giving 'partial credit'?" Some believe that "rubric" is a fancy, new-age euphemism for "partial credit." But these terms are, in fact, very different. When a teacher assigns partial credit, the process is essentially looking at the student work and deciding which pieces of the problem have been properly addressed. So, in the case of the shaded region problem, we might make the item worth a total of 6 points: 1 point for an attempt, 2 points for the correct process, 2 points for the final answer, 1 point for correctly identifying the units as square centimeters, or some similar scoring system. This process is often referred to as an *analytic* scoring process, where each step of the problem is analyzed and assigned a certain number of points toward a final grade.

The use of a rubric, on the other hand, is known as *holistic scoring*, because we view the "whole" student response and place the work on a particular level, according to a pre-established set of benchmarks. In the case of holistic scoring, we do not "check off" pieces of student work, as we recognize that there are multiple approaches to the problem and, therefore, no set list of items we are looking for in the answer anyway. And, if a student writes the final answer as 20 cm., instead of 20 sq. cm., the student will still score a "3" on the provided rubric, despite having an error in the units (unless units are a major consideration in the class, in which case, the teacher might choose to include "uses incorrect units" in the criteria for earning a "2").

Finally, keep in mind that rubric scores do *not* represent percentages. For example, if the student earns a "2" on the shaded area problem, it does not mean "2 out of 3 points" or 67%. In fact, in most school districts, 67% is either a D or an F, so a simple multiplication error could cause a potentially solid response to be viewed as a failure. Similarly, a "3" on a 4-point rubric does not imply that the student "got 75% correct." If a movie critic gives a film three stars on a five-star scale, it does not mean that 60% of the movie is excellent; it simply provides the viewer with a rating based on prescribed criteria, such as the quality of the script, acting, directing, editing, and so forth. So, when scoring a student paper on a rubric, the numbers represent a level of performance and communicate, to the student and the parent, how closely the response matches the stated criteria. Technically, a letter or word could be written on a student paper instead (such as "Excellent," "Fair," and so forth), but it is generally easier to use a number to represent the magnitude of a response. Most teachers tally rubric points over a grading period and scale them in some way to determine grades. This process of determining final grades will be described in the next chapter.

The other type of open-ended question is one in which there are weaker and stronger responses but not just one correct answer. In this case, we cannot have a "key" with an anticipated correct answer because there are a variety of solutions that are possible for the question. Consider the following example that could be asked in an algebra or integrated secondary mathematics class:

Give the equation of a very wide parabola whose vertex is a maximum that is not at the origin or on an axis. Then, describe your parabola and explain which features in your equation affect its shape, location, and orientation.

There are, of course, infinitely many equations that meet the stated criteria and several levels of depth at which students might provide the description. An example of a high-scoring response to this question might be:

Stephanie's Response

The equation is $y = -\frac{1}{5}(x-4)^2 + 7$. In this case, the vertex (also the maximum) is located at (4, 7). The negative coefficient on the quadratic term ($-\frac{1}{5}x^2$ would be the quadratic term if it is multiplied out) makes the parabola turn upside down (does not hold water). A small number such as $\frac{1}{5}$ serving as a coefficient makes the parabola much wider than if it was, say, a positive integer.

A much weaker response to the same question is illustrated in Danielle's answer:

Danielle's Response

I found the equation to be $y = 3(x-1)^2 - 4$. The "3" makes the parabola very wide. It would have to be, like, $y = 3x^2$ to have its vertex at the origin, so the "-1" and "-4" move it over from the origin.

Clearly, Stephanie's response is excellent and demonstrates a solid understanding of how the parameters in a quadratic equation affect the graph of the related parabola. She recognizes the effects of a negative quadratic coefficient whose absolute value is less than 1 and can correctly state the coordinates of the vertex of the parabola. Danielle's response, on the other hand, is fairly vague and illustrates some misunderstanding of the underlying mathematics. She does not "completely miss" the question, as she is able to explain the difference between an equation of a parabola with its vertex at the origin versus one which has been translated. However, she provides an incorrect explanation of the effect of using "3" as a coefficient and appears to ignore the issue of which way the parabola is oriented. And, while her equation does represent a parabola with its vertex somewhere other than the origin, she never provides the coordinates of the translated vertex.

Suppose you were to construct a rubric for scoring the answers to this open-ended question. And let's assume that your district (or your intuition) suggests the use of a 4-point rubric (five levels, with "0" being the lowest score). It is generally easiest to start off with the criteria for a "4" and ask yourself, "If a paper is going to be considered *excellent* (like Stephanie's), what are the necessary characteristics to earn the highest score?" Notice that a "4" does not mean that the paper is necessarily *perfect* — after all, students earn A's in classes all the time without averaging 100%. Nonetheless, this descriptor defines what are likely to be the best papers in the pile. Here is a possible narrative:

4 (*Excellent*)

The student provides a quadratic equation that has all of the three necessary components: (a) the vertex as a maximum, (b) the vertex somewhere other than the origin or an axis, and (c) a coefficient whose absolute value is small enough to suggest a wide parabola. The explanation thoroughly and correctly describes the parameters of the equation and how they impact the graph.

Now, let's look at Danielle's response. On a 4-point scale, where a "1" is nothing more than an attempt, and a "4" is as described here, where would you place this paper? If you are like most people, you'd have a hard time saying that the student merely "attempted" the question since she did at least know the general form for a quadratic equation and enough about it to know how the vertex is impacted by parameter changes. So, the student earned higher than a "1" but certainly doesn't meet the "4" criteria either. Perhaps a "2" could be used for Danielle to represented partial understanding of the problem. Extrapolating from the criteria for a "2," we can construct the criteria for the remainder of the rubric:

3 (Good)

The student provides a quadratic equation that has all of the three necessary components, but the explanation either neglects or incorrectly explains one or two of the parameters. OR the equation contains an error (such as forgetting the negative quadratic term coefficient), but the explanation of how the parameters affect the graph is consistent and clear.

2 (Fair/Partial Answer)

The student makes at least one mistake in the equation *and* makes an error or errors in the discussion of how parameters affect the graph. The student may also provide a correct and reasonable equation but no explanation, as required. Some understanding of the concept is evident, but the answer contains some significant flaws.

1 (Attempted/Needs Work)

The student made a reasonable attempt at the problem but has several major errors. For example, the equation may be quadratic, but the parameters are not adequately addressed. OR the student may have an incorrect equation but provide something in the explanation that indicates minimal knowledge of quadratic equations.

0 (No Response)

The student left the item blank or wrote down something that appears to be nothing more than copying down the given information or diagram.

It is also important to keep in mind that, just as there are high A's and low A's, there are high 4's and low 4's. When papers are scored for standardized tests, they are frequently read by two independent graders, each of whom places the paper on the rubric. If one person scores the response as a "3," while the other scores it as a "2," then the student is given a "2.5." However, as an individual teacher, we simply try to identify the category whose description most closely matches that of the student paper. Students, then, are not competing against one another; instead, they are trying to perform on a scale where the criteria are clearly detailed.

As you get used to asking open-ended questions on a regular basis, you will find the questions being easier to write and the rubric becoming simpler to define. Teachers often report that the use of rubrics is more time-consuming at first, but after some experience, they can actually grade papers faster than they could in the past. The holistic nature of scoring is generally easier than picking through the response for specific points (as is the case with partial credit or analytic scoring). Let's take a look at a few sample open-ended questions and some tips on how to write them.

One of the easiest ways to compose open-ended questions is to take a traditional question and modify it. The question can be adapted by providing the student with a scenario or by simply requesting an explanation. Figure 3.2 illustrates three examples of rewritten questions:

FIGURE 3.2. COMPARISON OF TRADITIONAL AND OPEN-ENDED QUESTIONS

TRADITIONAL QUESTION	MODIFIED OPEN-ENDED VERSION
Find 35% of 80.	Emily went to the store to buy a dress for the dance. She picked one that was marked $80, but the store was running a sale for "35% off" the regular price. She only brought a $50 bill. Will she have enough money for the dress? Why or why not?
Multiply: $(x + 7)^2$	Nick multiplied $(x + 7)^2$ and incorrectly got an answer of $x^2 + 49$. Explain where he made his mistake.
Find the length of a diagonal in a rectangle measuring 8 by 4.	Suppose that you had a round mirror with a diameter of 9 feet 6 inches. Can you fit it through a doorway measuring 4 feet wide and 8 feet high? Show your work and explain how you arrived at your answer.

Notice that the questions in the left-hand column of Figure 3.2 represent the traditional versions of typical middle and high school mathematics problems. They are "closed" in that they each have one, acceptable, correct answer. They are also skill-based and require no explanations. The right-hand column, by contrast, contains a modified version of each question. These problems are open-ended, and while each has an expected, correct answer (e.g., Emily will be at least $2 short for paying for the dress), each also requires some type of explanation. The quality of writing and explanation for the open-ended questions can be assessed by using a rubric describing possible levels of student responses. These questions emphasize more than correct answers and help the student to develop problem-solving, reasoning, and communication skills. In the first and third example, the skill was nested in a real-life scenario with an explanation required. In the second example, a fictitious student response was created, and the task of the person answering the question is to explain the error. This strategy of creating a sample student response and having others comment on it has become very popular in recent years. For example, if a teacher is trying to ensure that students understand the steps in the process of finding the slope of a line, the traditional item might say:

Find the slope of a line passing through the points $(5,9)$ *and* $(-10,12)$.

However, the open-ended version might read like this:

Brian was absent yesterday when we talked about the slope of a line. Write a letter to him that explains how to take the coordinates of two points such as $(5,9)$ *and* $(-10,12)$ *and use them to determine the slope. Include a diagram to prove that you understand* why *the procedure works.*

A common criticism of open-ended questions is that students are often being rewarded for wrong answers, even if the thinking processes are reasonable. However, we need to acknowledge that, perhaps, students *should* be getting some credit for understanding processes, despite having provided inaccurate answers. Also, answering the open-ended version of the slope problem is more difficult for many students than simply computing an answer in the traditional sense. So, we are not watering down the mathematics curriculum and our expectations; we are in effect *raising* expectations by using these types of questions. Again, the long-term impact should be to enhance the students' mathematical processing skills.

Here are some examples of 40 other open-ended mathematical questions. They have been grouped together by content area (Number and Operations, Algebra, Geometry, Measurement, Data Analysis and Probability), as suggested by the National Council of Teachers of Mathematics in *Principles and Standards for School Mathematics* (2000):

NUMBER AND OPERATIONS

♦ Draw a picture that shows why $\dfrac{3}{4} = \dfrac{6}{8}$.

♦ A fraction is written in the form $\dfrac{1}{n}$, where n can be any integer greater than 0. Explain what happens to the value of the fraction as n increases.

♦ Why do we "line up" the decimals when adding in a problem such as $2.49 + 3.108$?

♦ Do we get the same answer when we take 25% of 75 as when we take 75% of 25? Why or why not?

♦ Draw a diagram proving that $-3 - (-5) = 2$.

♦ Explain how a number is classified as rational or irrational. How can you tell the difference?

♦ How could you find $\sqrt{29}$ to the nearest hundredth if the square root button were broken on your calculator?

♦ What does it mean to say that the equation $x^2 + 25 = 0$ "has no Real roots?" Explain.

ALGEBRA

♦ What does it mean to say that "$x = -3$" is the solution to the equation $2(x + 5) - 10 = x - 3$?

♦ Make a drawing of algebra tiles that represent the following multiplication problem: $(x - 3)(x + 5) = x^2 + 2x - 15$.

♦ State the equations of two lines that are parallel and explain how you know that they are parallel.

♦ If a sugar cube is placed on a table, you can see 5 of its sides. When another cube is stacked on top of it, a total of 9 sugar cubes can be seen. How many sides can be seen when a third cube is stacked on top? a fourth? x cubes? Show or explain how you determined your answers.

♦ We have discussed that the shape of an absolute value graph is v-shaped. Given what you already know about the graphs of quadratic functions, predict what the graph of the following function would look like: $y = -4|x + 5| - 3$.

♦ Does the graph of $x = 4$ represent a function? Why or why not?

♦ Draw pictures and provide a brief explanation to show why some quadratic equations have two solutions, while others have only one solution, and some have none at all.

♦ Consider this equation: $10,000 = 2,000(1.065)^x$. Write a word problem that would require solving this equation for x to answer the question. Then, solve the equation and explain the meaning of your answer.

GEOMETRY

♦ "A square must be a rectangle, but a rectangle does not have to be a square." Is this statement true or false? Explain.

♦ Theresa said, "Any four-sided figure that has a right angle has to be a rectangle." Is she correct? How do you know?

♦ (Provide each student with a set of tangram pieces.) Select any 2 of the 7 tangram pieces and put them together to make as many different polygons as you can. Trace and label each polygon that you find.

♦ Make a list of all the properties of a rhombus you can think of.

♦ Sketch a diagram that shows why SSA is not a usable way to prove that two triangles are congruent.

♦ Do two figures that are congruent also have to be similar? Why or why not? (Be sure to include a diagram in your explanation.)

♦ Draw at least three possible nets for a cube.

♦ The formula for the sum of the interior angles in a polygon is $180(n-2)$. Draw a diagram and/or explain where this formula comes from.

MEASUREMENT

♦ (Provide each student a set of pattern blocks.) Which of the pattern block pieces has the greatest perimeter? the greatest area? How do you know?

♦ A quarter has a diameter of about 1 inch. If a million quarters were laid end-to-end, approximately how many miles long would the string of quarters be? Explain the process you used.

♦ Describe how you can quickly convert a temperature from Fahrenheit to Celsius in your head to get a rough estimate.

♦ Show how the formula for area of a circle follows naturally from the general formula that $A = \frac{1}{2} a \times p$, where a is the length of the apothem and p is the perimeter.

♦ Explain where the formula for volume of a cylinder ($V = \pi r^2 h$) came from by relating it to other volume formulas that you know.

♦ What happens to the area of a rectangle when the lengths of all of the sides are doubled? Draw a diagram and/or include an explanation to show how you know.

♦ Describe two different ways to determine the length of the hypotenuse in Figure 3.3.

FIGURE 3.3. OPEN-ENDED GEOMETRY QUESTION

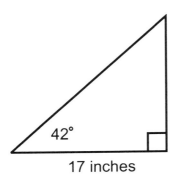

♦ Suppose that a quadrilateral contains a right angle and two angles with a measure of 63° each. (a) Find the measure of the remaining angle. (b) Explain if the remaining angle is right, obtuse, or acute and how you know.

DATA ANALYSIS AND PROBABILITY

♦ If four fair coins are tossed at the same time, are you more likely to get 2 Heads and 2 Tails or 1 Head and 3 Tails? Explain your reasoning.

♦ How many ways can 3 vases be lined up on a fireplace mantle? 4 vases? 5 vases? x vases? Explain the pattern that you see.

♦ Explain why the number of ways to choose 2 items from a group of 10 (C_2^{10}) must be equal to the number of ways to choose 8 items from the group of 10 (C_8^{10}).

♦ Would the "average" height of a person in our class be best reported as a mean, a mode, or as a median? How do you know?

♦ After taking a pot of boiling water off the burner, its temperature is recorded every 5 minutes. When graphing the data, would it be more appropriate to use a circle graph, a line graph, or a bar graph? Why?

♦ Suppose that the mode *and* the mean for a set of test scores in a class was 83%. Terry claims that if the students retake the test, and each member of the class scores exactly 5 points lower, neither the median nor the mean will change. Is he correct? Explain how you know.

♦ Consider the graph shown in Figure 3.4. What does the graph tell you? What does the graph *not* tell you? Explain how you know.

FIGURE 3.4. CANDY SALE BAR GRAPH

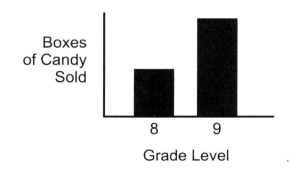

♦ The probability of a manufacturer making a defective container is 1 in 1,000. If 999 containers in a row have been made without having a defect, what is the probability that the 1000th container will be defective? Explain.

For each of these 40 questions, a specific rubric could be developed with which to evaluate student responses. Often, school districts have a *generalized rubric* that is pre-established, whose descriptors are not connected to any particular question, as illustrated in Chapter 2 (a general rubric from 0 to 4 was presented). From there, teachers can tailor the rubric to fit specific questions raised on homework assignments, in-class writing, or tests so that they contain the detail shown in this chapter. Some districts and tests prefer a simple rubric of 0-2 (Incorrect Response, Partial Response, Correct Response), while others have as much as a 10-point scale on which to assess responses. Most teachers find that a rubric with 4 or 5 levels of performance is the most realistic. The rubric with 4 or 5 levels has enough detail to differentiate between high and low performances but is not so detailed that it becomes difficult to distinguish performance levels for two given papers. In the end, each teacher needs to try out some open-ended questions and a couple of different rubrics until one style feels comfortable. From there, students, parents, and teachers alike will begin to rely on the rubric to provide valuable feedback on the quality of student responses. Often, open-ended questions are used as prompts for journal writing. In the next section, we take up the issue of using journals in the mathematics classroom and the logistics of using that strategy.

SAMPLE JOURNAL PROMPTS

While journals have been used for decades in the Language Arts classroom, they are relatively new to the field of teaching and learning mathematics. Generally, mathematics teachers have students keep a spiral notebook or binder that is separate from their class notebooks, into which they can write responses to questions or complete thoughts that are generated by the teacher. These questions are called *prompts*. Suppose, for example, that a class has a large number of questions on a homework assignment from the previous day. The teacher might ask the students to take out their journals and complete this thought: "The most difficult homework problem for me was . . . because . . . " This prompt pushes students to reflect on their work and to identify the factors that got in the way of understanding the assignment. For example, one student might note that a particular problem was difficult because he didn't know what the question was asking, while another student may state that she understood the question but didn't understand the algebraic steps well enough to complete her work.

After doing an activity where students measured the circumferences and diameters of several round objects, such as lids and canisters, a sixth grade class discovered a formula for determining the circumference of a circle when the radius was given. The teacher, in turn, asked the class to explain how one can go about finding the circumference of a circle in their journals. In her journal entry, Colleen stated:

If you know the radius, here is what you do –

1) Multiply it by 2 to get the diameter (unless you have the diameter and don't have to change it).

2) Multiply this number by 3.14 which is about the value of pi.

3) Round the answer to two decimal places.

Interestingly, Colleen was never *given* a procedure for determining the circumference of a circle. She developed and explained her three-step procedure based on her classroom observations, with no direct input from the teacher. In a sense, the journal was the tool that allowed her to reflect on the day's lesson and to put her understanding of the formula for circumference into her own words. The teacher, then, can read Colleen's entry to see if she has grasped the concept, to determine whether any misconceptions arose, and to decide if any further intervention will be necessary.

In a high school classroom, the teacher asked the students to compare the study of mathematics to an animal and explain their thinking. The following examples are taken from actual student journal entries in the class. Enrique wrote:

> *If I think of mathematics as an animal, I believe it is most like a snake. Snakes are very frightening to look at, but very few can really hurt you at all. Math is like that — sometimes a problem or a chapter can look scary, but once you start to actually do it, you find out that it's not really so hard after all. Too many people are scared off from studying math because it "looks" so hard. They don't give it enough of a chance, just like people will run from a snake that is perfectly harmless.*

In the same class, Michelle's journal entry was the following:

> *If math were an animal, it would most likely be a turtle. It would be a turtle because a turtle has a hard outer shell. Just like a math problem, because it can be very hard sometimes to figure the answer out. However, inside, under the shell is very soft. Just like when you start a math problem, it seems very hard, but once you get into it it's very easy.*

After reading Enrique and Michelle's journal entries, the teacher realized that they had some fear of mathematics, yet they both were aware that many mathematics problems appear to be far more difficult to solve than they are after expending some effort. The teacher, in turn, decided to focus some lessons on problem-solving experiences that would enhance the confidence level of the students, while trying to develop the disposition of perseverance necessary to solve difficult problems. The entries provided a rich window on student thinking that would not have been possible without the use of the assessment tool.

Teachers use journals in the mathematics classroom for a variety of purposes, such as the following:

♦ *Problem Solving* — Students can be periodically given problems to solve as their journal prompts. By reading their solutions, teachers can identify thinking patterns in students as they reason out the problems. Open-ended problems serve as excellent prompts in this area, as students are challenged to try to solve a difficult problem and explain their thinking in the journals. In this way, journal entries can be used to support the skill of responding to open-ended questions; thus, the two assessment strategies go hand-in-hand.

♦ *Reactions to Classwork or Homework* — As teachers, we are interested to know how students are reacting to activities we do in class, as well as problems assigned for homework. Students can be asked to reflect on a classroom situation, describe the characteristics of each person who worked with them on a team project, or summarize their learning from a particular assignment. Without this type of journal entry, the teacher only sees the "work" of the students — their final products — as opposed to accessing their thinking about the effectiveness of classroom activities and homework problems.

♦ *Self-Assessment of Work* — One of the most difficult — yet most important — skills that students need to develop in school is the ability to recognize quality work when they or someone else produces it. William Glasser, a noted psychologist and author, wrote about the importance of self-assessment in his book, *The Quality School* (1990). He stated that students should "assess the quality of the work that others do and . . . discuss how they came to their conclusions. It is from these discussions that students get a tangible idea of what quality is and what has to be done to achieve it . . . When there is a difference between the student's and the teacher's assessment of the quality of an assignment or test, the teacher should discuss the difference with the student. From these discussions students learn to judge what determines quality work" (pp. 64-65). Many teachers take advantage of the journal as a tool to get students to reflect on their own work or the work of others. For example, students can be asked to write about how they studied for a particular test (e.g., how long they studied, what part of the day, where they did the studying, whether they talked to friends, etc.) and how they would study differently if they had the test to do over again. Students, like teachers, will only improve their performance if they recognize their shortcomings and can set goals to overcome them.

♦ *Goal Setting* — At the beginning of a new chapter, unit, or quarter, students can be asked to set one or more goals for the next time period and then, later, reflect on the degree to which they accomplished those goals. For example, one student might set a goal to participate more actively in class, while another student decides to use study hall time more effectively to seek help while in school. Simple, attainable goal setting can help students develop as learners and become more organized.

♦ *Autobiographies and Stories* — Some mathematics teachers take advantage of the opportunity to connect writing skills to the mathematics classroom. Students can be asked to write an autobiography of what it was like to be a mathematics student over the years since entering a particular class. During the school year, they can be asked to use mathematical terms in short stories that they creatively compose in their journals. These autobiographies and stories can be very helpful in understanding student thinking and appreciating their ways of viewing the world.

♦ *Instructional Suggestions* — This area is often the most difficult for many teachers. But students generally possess very helpful suggestions on how to make a mathematics class more interesting and worthwhile. Teachers can ask students to describe, for example, the greatest strength of a class, what they would like to see improved in the class, and how they might suggest making the class better. Common threads of student thinking can lead to improvement of the learning environment and, ultimately, an increase in student performance. Of course, the use of this type of journal entry depends on the teacher's willingness to take constructive criticism and the students' comfort with expressing their honest opinions to the teacher. As such, this is not the type of journal entry that a teacher might request in the first couple of months of the school year but can be very helpful in refining and improving the classroom routine for the second half of the school year.

Here are some examples of 32 "general" journal prompts that can be used at virtually any grade level. They can be used "as is," adapted to local needs, or serve as a model for additional questions that students might be asked to respond to in a journal entry:

1. Write a Mathematics Autobiography that describes your experiences in mathematics classes over the years, how you feel today, and the type of mathematics you expect to be studying five years from now.
2. "This week in math class I learned . . . "
3. "I wish we had spent more time in the chapter on . . . because . . . "
4. "The best experience in this class for me this quarter was . . . "
5. "The easiest homework problem for me last night was . . . because . . . "
6. "If mathematics were an animal, it would be a(n) . . . because . . . "
7. "This week I am going to try harder to . . . "
8. "When I do work with the other students at my table, I feel . . ."
9. "In class, I like it best when the teacher . . . "
10. "In class, I wish that the teacher would . . . because . . . "

11. "When we did the problem in class today, we solved it by . . . but another way to solve the same problem would have been to . . . "

12. "The main point of today's math lesson was . . . "

13. "When I studied for my test, I spent most of my time . . . "

14. "After looking my graded test over, I now realize that . . . "

15. "My goal for the Second Quarter is to . . . "

16. "Today in class I felt . . . because . . . "

17. "No matter how hard the teacher has tried, I am still confused by . . . "

18. "My greatest strength as a mathematics student is that I . . . "

19. Write a letter to a person who was absent from class and explain to that student how to do what we learned in class today.

20. Design two test questions for the next test. Provide solutions and explain why you think they would make good test questions.

21. "The problem we solved today is a lot like the problem where . . . because . . . "

22. "I'm really proud of the fact that I . . . "

23. "Sometimes, I wonder . . . "

24. "If I had this week of mathematics class to do over again, I wish I would have . . . "

25. "An interesting mathematical issue that I saw in the newspaper this past week was . . . " (attach a copy of the article)

26. Compose three word problems like the one that we solved in class today and provide a solution for each.

27. "When I use a calculator to solve this kind of problem, I . . . "

28. "My opinion about using algebra tiles to multiply polynomials is that . . ."

29. "The most interesting problem we solved this quarter was . . . because . . . "

30. "A site I found on the Internet that can be useful in learning mathematics is . . . "

31. Write an algorithm (a step-by-step procedure) for how to . . . (factor a polynomial, divide decimals, use the Pythagorean Theorem to find a triangle side length, etc.)

32. Define a mathematical term in your own words, providing an example and/or a picture.

Of course, almost any mathematical problem — preferably, open-ended in nature — can serve as an effective journal prompt. The purpose of the journal is to challenge students to reflect on problems, solutions to problems, or classroom teaching and learning strategies. The journals allow a teacher to "get to know" the students much more closely than is possible through classroom interactions alone. Many students, for example, are shy in class and are slow to respond to class-wide questions. But those same students will freely express their thinking and reasoning in a journal, opening up new avenues for the teacher to reach out to each individual. Also, since the process of reflection leads to the advancement of mathematical thinking, students will often sort out and make sense of mathematics through writing in the journal (such as the student did when devising three steps for finding the circumference of a circle). Often, they can have an "aha" experience *while writing the journal entry* that helps the students to crystallize an idea or concept through the writing process. In a classroom that promotes mathematical processes — Problem Solving, Reasoning and Proof, Communication, Connections, and Representation, as recommended by the NCTM (2000) — it makes sense that the teacher would use tools such as journals that advance the students' ability to "do" mathematics.

As was discussed in Chapter 2, some teachers see the collection and reading of journals as a burden, as it can be very time-consuming. However, the time spent reading journal responses can far outweigh the time a teacher often spends going back over topics after students perform poorly on a test, exhibiting misconceptions that the teacher did not know existed prior to the test. In short, the journals can serve as a useful aid to track student thinking and to look for ongoing, class-wide patterns of performance. Ultimately, the comments that students write in journals can and should impact classroom teaching methods. You will have to decide for yourself whether it is best to give students a journal prompt each day, twice a week, once a week, or some other timeframe that makes sense to you.

Another common concern is how to "grade" journal entries when reading student work. There are three different approaches that one might use for assessing student work in a journal. Some teachers, for example, do not "grade" journals at all but simply have students write in them during class time and read them periodically to gain feedback. As such, the journals do not affect final grades at all and serve as an ungraded way to gather informal data about students. However, this approach may not motivate the students to do their best work, as we have already discussed how they generally perform best when the work "counts" toward a grade.

Another approach used by some teachers is to base a journal grade upon the number of completed entries. For example, let's suppose that the teacher assigns three journal writing prompts per week and collects the journals every two weeks — five journal collections for the quarter. If the journal is collected, and the student has done a reasonable job of addressing all of the prompts over the two weeks, then the student receives full credit for that journal collection. Suppose, then, that the student gets full credit 4 out of 5 times during the quarter. In this case, the student would receive an 80% as a journal grade for the quarter. This grading policy does not account for "par-

RUBRIC FOR SCORING JOURNALS
Advanced Eighth Grade Mathematics

3 = Excellent

♦ all journal entries assigned in class have been completed

♦ journal prompts assigned in class have been properly addressed in entries

♦ entries are insightful and well-written

♦ journal is organized, properly labeled (dates and day numbers), and easy to read (i.e., handwriting is legible)

♦ evidence of excellent mathematical reasoning and communication skills are exhibited

2 = Acceptable

♦ all journal entries assigned in class have been completed

♦ most journal prompts have been properly addressed in entries

♦ entries are sufficient but may lack insight; some entries may be too short to show depth

♦ journal is fairly organized but may lack proper labeling (dates and day numbers) or be somewhat difficult to read (i.e., illegible handwriting)

♦ evidence of good mathematical reasoning and communication skills are exhibited

1 = Needs Work or Incomplete

♦ journal has been turned in but may be missing 1-2 required entries

♦ some journal prompts may not be properly addressed

♦ entries generally lack insight; many entries may be too short to show any depth

♦ journal is disorganized, may be poorly labeled, and is difficult to read (illegible)

♦ little, if any, evidence of mathematical reasoning and communication skills are exhibited

0 = Not Turned In or Unacceptable

♦ journal was not turned in at all OR was missing more than 2 required entries and, therefore, unacceptable

♦ journal prompts have not been properly addressed or were not addressed at all

♦ included entries are too short to show any depth

♦ journal is very disorganized, poorly-labeled, and handwriting is almost illegible

♦ evidence of mathematical reasoning and communication skills is lacking

tial credit"; if the student did not complete all 6 of the required entries for a given two-week period, no credit is given for that collection period. The system is fairly simple in terms of grading: The teacher merely needs to look over the student journal, determine whether an adequate attempt was done for each journal collection, and place a "check" or a "0" in the grade book. As we know, however, there are students who do "adequate" work but others who do "outstanding" work, while others get a "0" for doing 5 out of 6 entries properly. So, the third system used by some teachers is a scoring rubric for journal writing.

Borrowing from the notion of scoring rubrics for open-ended questions, a teacher can devise a set of benchmarks for journal performance and then use that rubric to score the journals at each collection period. On the previous page is an example of a rubric that is being used by a high school mathematics teacher.

Notice that the rubric presented is general enough to be used at any level for any mathematics course. Yet it provides enough detail to clearly communicate expectations to students and allow for fairly accurate, objective assessing of student work. As a teacher becomes familiar with this rubric, the process of scoring student work can become as automatic and rapid as grading with a "check" or a "0," but this method provides the students with considerably more input about the quality of their work. Parents will also appreciate the fact that each number represents a category and that descriptors set a list of expectations for the student.

Some teachers find it much easier to use a simple rubric such as the following:

2	Complete and insightful
1	Complete but needs more depth
0	Incomplete

Again, the assessment process depends on personal preference of the teacher, which may also be a function of experience and comfort with using rubrics. If you have never used journals or rubrics before, it may make sense to begin with a simple rubric until defining your own performance standards and then building a more detailed rubric over some period of time. Students themselves can be helpful in defining what constitutes a "good" journal entry and may be involved in the rubric writing process. Converting rubric points to percentages for the determination of final grades will be described in some detail in Chapter 4. Next, we will turn our attention to the use of long- and short-term projects and student presentations as an assessment strategy.

SAMPLE PROJECTS AND PRESENTATIONS

Ideally, the mathematics classroom should mirror "real life" experiences in problem solving. And the truth is that most real world problems are fairly complicated and cannot be solved in a few minutes with a single calculation or procedure. When the emphases in the classroom include problem solving and communication, it follows that students should be expected to explore complex problems and present their results to peers. Teachers, in turn, can capture the quality of work produced on these projects to assess student progress. One teacher, for example, took her class on a Math Trail at the end of a unit on measurement. The Trail was a field trip around the downtown area in which students had to determine the areas of parking lots, estimate the heights of several buildings, and measure the angles of adjoining glass pieces in stained glass windows. Then, each team of students was required to present its findings to the class, together with a discussion of the processes used to solve the problems. The project counted the same as a test grade but involved an afternoon of field trip work and a day of presentations.

Projects can take on a variety of formats, depending on the comfort level of the teacher and the needs of the students. For example, some projects are done individually, while others are done in pairs or small groups (learning teams). Sometimes, the students present their findings to the whole class; other times, they present to small groups within the class, and in other situations, they submit a written paper with no presentation at all. In addition, the projects can be assessed in several ways. Some teachers use a holistic rubric to score a project, for example, while others assign a certain number of points for each part of the project and tally the points earned to determine the final grade (an analytic scoring process). Classroom interactions and presentations may or may not be included as part of the formal assessment of student work. Six project ideas will be described here, together with a detailed presentation of how a teacher can assess student work for each. They will serve as field-tested exemplars of the type of projects that students can be asked to do across the middle and secondary grade levels.

FUNCTIONS LEARNING STATIONS PROJECT — PATTERNS, ALGEBRA

This three-day project outlined on the next page can be given to middle or secondary students as they learn to write the equations of linear functions with data they have collected and analyzed.

The students then circulate between six learning stations at a pace of three stations per day, with each station providing an activity and a problem, such as the following (these station activities can vary, depending on the grade level and course of study):

◆ Each student is to draw six different right triangles on a sheet of paper and use a protractor to measure each angle. (The triangles may not be congruent or similar to one another.) The two acute angle measures should be recorded

FUNCTIONS LEARNING STATIONS PROJECT

Purpose:

The purpose of this three-day project is twofold: (1) You will gain additional experiences with exploring linear functions as they occur in the world, and (2) your ability to apply the function concept to solving problems can be assessed and evaluated.

Process:

On the first two days of the project, teams of 3 or 4 will circulate among six learning stations (three per day). At each station, you will explore a function by hand, with a graphing calculator, or both. You will also be expected to answer questions and draw conclusions at each station. Any of the three problems that are not completed at the end of each day must be finished as a homework assignment. You are responsible for choosing your own teams for this project.

On the third and final day of the project, you will compare final results to each learning station's questions and choose "best" solutions to be submitted for grades. The following rules apply:

♦ only one "version" per team from each learning station is to be submitted for grading

♦ the six solutions should be stapled together with a post-it note on the front page identifying the team members

♦ each team member <u>must</u> contribute at least one solution to the final product. The name of the person whose paper is being submitted for grading should be identified on the problem page.

Assessment:

The project will be scored on an 80-point scale (which will be converted to a percentage) and will count in the "Projects" portion of this quarter's grades. The 80 points will be determined as follows:

<u>60 points</u> = 10 points maximum for each of the six learning centers. Scores will be based on quality and accuracy of responses and clarity/neatness of work.

<u>20 points</u> = up to 20 points will be awarded to each student for participation and contributions to the team effort. This score will be determined from two sources: (1) You will be observed during problem solving over the three days, and notes will be taken on your skills at Problem Solving, Communicating, Reasoning, Connecting, and Representing Mathematics. (2) You will each rate one another's participation on the last day, providing input for one another's grades.

Teacher's Role:

My role in this project is to set up the learning centers and to observe your work. I will not answer questions as to whether or not a team is on the "right track," etc. Your problem solving strategies and accuracy are up to you.

Good luck!

as ordered pairs and graphed. The student looks for a line of best fit for these points and describes the meaning of the equation.

♦ Each team of students sits down at a station that includes several walnut wooden cubes (each measuring one cubic inch), several balsa wood cubes of the same size, and a balance. Determining the weight of one cube, then two, then three, and so on, students draw a graph relating the number of cubes (x) to the total weight (y). After doing this for both the walnut and balsa wood, the students compare the equations and determine how the density of the wood affects the slope of each line. (Actually, the slope of each line *is* the density!)

♦ Students are reminded that the freezing and boiling points of water in Fahrenheit are 32° and 212°, respectively, while the Celsius equivalents are 0° and 100°. Students are to use these facts to write an equation relating Fahrenheit to Celsius that one could use to convert between systems.

♦ Provide students with a listing of the cost of a first-class postage stamp from over the years (see Figure 3.5). Ask them to draw a graph where the year is the independent variable, and the cost is the dependent variable. Then, students should find a line of best fit to make a prediction of the cost of a postage stamp in 10 years.

FIGURE 3.5. COST OF POSTAGE STAMPS SINCE 1974

YEAR	COST OF POSTAGE STAMP
1974	10¢
1975	13¢
1978	15¢
1981	18¢
1985	22¢
1994	29¢
1995	32¢
1999	33¢
2001	34¢

♦ Provide students with tape measures and several circular objects. They should measure each object and record its diameter on the horizontal axis and its circumference on the vertical axis. Drawing a line of best fit, students should be able to find its equation and explain how the slope of the line becomes an approximation for the value of π.

♦ At one station, students are given a stopwatch, a ruler, and a birthday candle. They are to light the candle and measure its height every 5 seconds. After collecting the data, the can plot the points (where the independent variable is time, and the dependent variable is height) on a graphing calculator and determine a line of best fit. Students should determine that the slope of the line describes the rate at which the candle burns. (NOTE: Caution should be taken to ensure that students are safely burning the candle, as would be the case if they were doing a similar activity in a science lab.)

As students work on this project, the role of the teacher is to observe their performances and make notes on a clipboard about each student's ability to problem solve, reason, communicate, connect, and represent functions mathematically. Each student is assigned a score for participation (out of 20 points), and the entire team earns a score on the solutions themselves (60 points) for a project grade based on an 80-point scale.

REAL-LIFE FUNCTIONS PROJECT — FUNCTIONS, ALGEBRA

Students at the middle school or secondary levels are given one week to do this project on an individual basis (see project description and assessment form on the following pages). Each student is responsible for identifying, representing, and explaining an example of an authentic situation involving functions as they appear in the student's life.

After giving the students one week of working time, the teacher collects all of the project papers and has each student make a five-minute presentation to the class. As students make presentations in class, the teacher uses the form provided for assessment

The teacher then grades the paper on a 70-point scale (analytically, with each section of the paper being worth about 8-10 points) and converts the 20 points on the Presentation Form to a 30-point scale to equal a total of 100 possible points.

REAL-LIFE FUNCTIONS PROJECT

Rationale:

The purpose of this project is to get you to apply some of the concepts of functions to a real-life situation of your own.

Timeline:

The written paper is due one week from today, and presentations will begin on that day.

Assessment:

This short project will "count" the same weight as a test score of 100 points, as follows:

  70 points — Written Paper

  30 points — Presentation to Class

Requirements:

Each person is to come up with one, real-life example of a function that affects you or your family. Do not "make up" a fictitious function — we want a <u>real</u> example of a function you encounter in your life. You may want to discuss this with your parents to come up with a good example to use. Then, in a paper, you are to "write up" the following eight items:

A. Explain/Describe the function that you selected and include <u>why</u> you selected it (e.g., "My parents have a voicemail service, so I chose a function that related the monthly cost of the service to the number of messages left on voicemail. I knew that the monthly fee was $8.00 and that each call cost 50¢ ...").

B. Explain which variable is independent, which is dependent and <u>explain how you know</u>.

C. Create a table showing several values that relate the variables.

D. Draw an accurately, fully labeled graph of the function on an attached piece of graph paper.

E. Write a verbal statement of your relationship using the expression "is a function of" in your statement.

F. Find a recursive formula that describes your function.

G. Find a closed (explicit) formula <u>and</u> an equation (using y and x) that describes your function.

H. Determine whether your function is discrete or continuous and <u>explain how you know</u>.

Then, in class, on your assigned day, you are to present your project to the class and provide us with an overview of your function. You have about 5 minutes to make your presentation, and you will be assessed on your ability to accurately explain and describe the function you studied. Most effective presentations include some kind of visual, so you might want to use the overhead graphing calculator or make a poster to help the class visualize your function.

ORAL PRESENTATION ASSESSMENT FORM

Name: _____

Class Presentation:

	1 (Low)	2	3	4 (High)
Presentation	——	——	——	——
Knowledge of Function	——	——	——	——
Quality of Explanation	——	——	——	——
Use/Quality of Visual Aid	——	——	——	——
Communication Skills (including grammar, etc.)	——	——	——	——

Comments:

SCORE = _____ out of 20 points

GRAPHING PROJECT — GRAPHS, FUNCTIONS, ALGEBRA, GEOMETRY/ TRANSLATIONS

In this project, secondary or middle school students explore the graphs of a variety of functions on a graphing calculator to generalize and make conjectures about the graphs of other functions. Students are arranged into teams of three or four, with responsibilities for each student specified in the instructions. In the end, each team generates a presentation, a written paper, and a piece of artwork.

GRAPHING PROJECT

Rationale:

We have discovered that the graph of the equation $y = x$ is a line, that changing the coefficient of x changes the slope, and that adding/subtracting a number to/from the product changes the y-intercept of the line. All of these lines are created "equal" but experience subtle changes as the parameters are changed. In this project, you will be studying several other families of graphs. Each team of 3 or 4 members will be asked to explore one family.

Families to Be Studied:

$$y = x^2,\ y = x^3,\ y = x^4,\ y = |x|,\ y = \sqrt{x}\ ,\ y = \frac{1}{x},\ y = \sqrt[3]{x}$$

Team Member Roles:

Facilitator   This is the person who is in charge of the exploration process, makes sure that the writer and artist understand and are doing their tasks, and presents the results of the work to the class. The quality of the classroom presentation will be included in the grade. If your team has four members, it will have two co-facilitators who will present the information to the class as a pair.

Writer   This is the person who is responsible for taking the notes as the team explores its graphs. Then, when all of the exploration has taken place, the Writer is responsible for producing the written document that the team will submit.

Artist   This is the person who designs and makes the posterboard artwork that summarizes the findings of the group. The board may contain graphs, written statements, or whatever the team and the artist feel best represents the results of the exploration in picture form. The poster will be submitted at the time of the class's presentation.

Process:

The assignment will begin with an exploration in class on Monday. Teams will be given some class time each day so that they can discuss their work and produce the presentation, written document, and artwork by the end of the week.

Assessment:

The grade on this project will carry the weight of a regular test score. Grades will include individual and team components as explained below:

1. Each team member will be graded individually by the teacher on his/her ability to work with other students. Notes will be taken by the teacher during exploration time, and each student will receive a score between 0 and 10 on his/her ability to problem-solve, reason, communicate, connect, and represent the mathematics.

2. At the end of the project, everyone will fill out self-evaluations of the team's willingness and ability to work together. Essentially, you will be responsible for grading the other team members' contribution to the project effort. From this evaluation and student input, each person will receive a score between 0 and 10.

3. Each team will receive a grade for the quality of the classroom presentation. The presentation should not only include an explanation but should *involve* the class in the exploration (for example, students could be asked to "draw" a couple of graphs with their graphing calculators during the presentation). The presentation should be planned to take about 15 minutes and will be videotaped. From this presentation, the Presenter will receive a score between 0 and 15.

4. Each team will receive a grade for the quality of the paper presented. The paper should summarize the findings of the team as the exploration was conducted. It may include a few drawings; typed papers will be scored higher than hand-written papers. The paper must be submitted when the presentation is given to the class. From this paper, the Writer will receive a score between 0 and 15 points.

5. Each team will receive a grade for the quality of the poster created. The poster should summarize the findings of the group in pictorial terms. It may include pictures, examples, or whatever the artist and team choose to display. The poster must be submitted when the presentation is given to the class. From this poster, the artist will receive a score between 0 and 15.

Each student has the potential to accumulate up to 35 points. Of the 35 points, 20 come from team-generated work, while 15 points are up to the individual student to earn. The score will then be converted to a percent to produce a grade on a 100-point scale.

It is important in this project that the three (or four) members of the team be given very specific requirements so that they have individual accountability for their work. The team works together as it gathers information, but in the end, each student has a product to generate and submit which counts for almost half of the grade on the project. During class time, students are given approximately 15–20 minutes each day to explore their function family and to collaborate on the contents of the paper, presentation, and artwork. At the end of the week, each student completes the following Self-Assessment Form, and the student feedback is used together with teacher notes to determine participation scores:

TEAM PROJECT SELF-ASSESSMENT FORM

Name: _____

Name of Team Member: _____

1 = Strongly Disagree, 2 = Disagree, 3 = Somewhat, 4 = Agree, 5 = Strongly Agree

Willing to help others on the team	1	2	3	4	5
Clearly communicates ideas to others	1	2	3	4	5
Demonstrates good problem-solving skills	1	2	3	4	5
Contributes significantly to the team effort	1	2	3	4	5

Letter grade you would give team member for his/her contribution: _____

Comments (required):

Students tend to be surprisingly honest when completing this type of form. A student can also be asked to fill out a form for him/herself as a Self-Assessment as well, and comparing these marks to those of the rest of the group can prove to be very revealing. The teacher should use the self-assessments in conjunction with observational notes taken during the project to determine students' final participation grades.

After the students have rated one another and made their presentations, the following form can be used to summarize the scores. A completed copy of this sheet would then be distributed to each student as a final assessment report:

GRAPHING PROJECT ASSESSMENT

Part I: Ability to work with others during team exploration time

Score: _____ (out of 10 possible points)

Comments:

Part II: Evaluation of your contribution to the group effort

Score: _____

Comments:

Part III: Assessment of Individual Work

Mathematical Content: _____ (out of 5 possible points)

Style/Appearance _____ (out of 5 possible points)

Preparation _____ (out of 5 possible points)

Comments:

Part IV: Total Points

TOTAL POINTS EARNED: _____ (out of 35 possible points)

PROJECT GRADE: _____

It is also important for the teacher to share all of the forms and rubrics with the students at the outset of the project so that the expectations are clear. Again, students can be involved in developing the scoring rubric themselves. When students take ownership in determining, for example, what a "good" piece of artwork looks like, they are more likely to form an image of quality work and what they need to do. Also, the "up front" and open sharing of rubrics and expectations allow the teacher to be very clear about what the project entails, reducing the possibility of students claiming later that they "didn't know what you wanted" or guessing as to the teacher's requirements. The notion of openness in assessment is emphasized in the NCTM *Assessment Standards for School Mathematics* (1995), which will be discussed further in Chapter 5.

ANALYTIC GEOMETRY PROJECT — COORDINATE GEOMETRY (PYTHAGOREAN THEOREM, SLOPE, DISTANCE, MIDPOINT)

Primarily designed for secondary mathematics students, this project involves the analysis of geometric figures through the use of formulas to determine slopes, parallel and perpendicular line relationships, distances, and midpoints. The students work together in class for one full class period to begin the problems, then are given a week to complete their individual work. Papers are collected and graded individually — essentially, students have been given the opportunity, both in class and outside of class, to help one another but are assessed for their own individual product.

ANALYTIC GEOMETRY PROJECT

Rationale:

Using the Pythagorean Theorem, Slope, and the Distance Formula, mathematicians can use algebra to prove theorems and show characteristics of geometric shapes. The purpose of this project is to get you to apply the algebra we have been using to the study of geometric shapes.

Process/Deadlines:

You are being assigned this project on Friday. You can work on it at your tables during class time on Monday. Then, your final set of solutions is due at the beginning of class on the following Monday.

Assessment:

Since each problem is to be sketched carefully on graph paper, you can then do your algebra work on the graph paper or on an attached sheet of looseleaf paper. An overall score on a scale of 1-10 will be given for neatness/accuracy of your work. Then, each problem will be worth 15 points so that the entire project is worth 100 points (the equivalent of one test score). Good luck!

Problems:

1. You should remember that a *rhombus* is a quadrilateral in which all four sides are congruent. Plot the following four points on graph paper: A = (0, 3), B = (3, 9), C = (9, 6), and D = (6, 0). Quadrilateral ABCD is a rhombus.

    (a) Prove that this is true by finding the lengths of AB, BD, DC, and AC and showing that they are all equal.

    (b) AC and BD are called *diagonals* of the rhombus. Determine whether the diagonals of this rhombus are congruent to one another.

2. Recall that when we find the <u>slope</u> of a line, we take the change in *y* divided by the change in *x* (rise over run).

    (a) Using the same diagram as for #1, calculate the slopes of AB, BC, CD, and AD. What do you notice about these slopes?

    (b) What type of figure, besides being a rhombus, does this relationship make the quadrilateral? How do you know?

3. Plot the following points to form Quadrilateral DEFG: D = (3, -2), E = (6, -3), F = (5, -6), and G = (2, -5).

    (a) Calculate the slopes of segments DE, EF, FG, and GD.

(b) What do these slopes tell you about how the sides of the figure are related?

(c) In order to fully classify the quadrilateral, we have to know more about the relationship of the lengths of the sides. Calculate the lengths of DE, EF, FG, and GD.

(d) Look at the lengths that you calculated in the last step and the answer to part (b) of this problem. How would you classify this quadrilateral, given all of the information that you have? How do you know?

4. Plot the following points to form Quadrilateral WXYZ: W = (-2, 5), X = (1, 7), Y = (5, 6), and Z = (-1, 2).

(a) Calculate the slopes of WX, XY, YZ, and ZW.

(b) What do these slopes tell you about how the sides of the figure are related?

(c) With this information, how would you classify this quadrilateral? How do you know?

(d) Determine the lengths of the diagonals. Are they congruent? Would they ever be congruent for this type of polygon? Why or why not?

5. Plot the following points to form Triangle PTR: P = (-5, 1), T = (-7, 4), and R = (-3, 4).

(a) Calculate the lengths of the three sides, PT, TR, and PR.

(b) How would you classify this acute triangle, based on the information from part (a)? How do you know?

(c) Using the lengths you calculated in part (a), show/prove why this must be an acute triangle.

6. A MIDPOINT is a point that is exactly halfway between two other given points. Plot the points A, B, and C on your graph paper, as follows: A = (-7, 0), B = (-2, 2), and C = (3, 4).

(a) Calculate the lengths of AB and BC. Compare them to determine whether or not B is the midpoint of segment AC.

(b) How could you use the coordinates of points A and C to find the coordinates of midpoint B? Generalize this — how could you find the coordinates of *any* midpoint if you are given the coordinates of the two endpoints of the line segment?

After the students have had a week to work on the six problems, the teacher collects all of the projects, and each person is assessed individually, using a scoring rubric for each of the items. Some students may seek the help of classmates more than others during the week, but the intent is for students to produce their best work and to do so outside of class time. This project can be used in place of a more traditional written "test" on coordinate geometry in a geometry, algebra, or pre-calculus course.

FRACTAL PROJECT — GEOMETRY, ALGEBRAIC EXPRESSIONS, ITERATION

After completing a series of lessons on fractal geometry, including the notion of beginning with a pre-fractal "seed" and applying a rule over and over (iterating), students can be challenged to generate their own fractal images. This is an individual project that can be done at the secondary level, in which students create a fractal image and describe it in a variety of ways. Students have one week to complete the work.

FRACTAL PROJECT

One week from today, each student will turn in one fractal image, created by hand and following some clearly defined rule of iteration. The following are required:

1. a **fractal image**, illustrating <u>at least</u> 3 iterations (more, if possible)
2. a **written description** of the seed and the rule used for iteration
3. a **problem**, created by the student, that can be solved using the fractal image
4. a **solution** to the problem, clearly and accurately solved

The following rubric or grading scale will be used to assess your work:

<u>30</u> *Basic Requirements* (30 points): A fractal image with a description and question with its solution have been submitted.

For the following criteria, this scale will be used:

5 = Outstanding
4 = Good
3 = Acceptable
2 = Fair
1 = Needs Work

<u>5</u> *Fractal Image* (1-5 points): The picture makes good use of color, is neatly drawn, displays at least the third stage, and shows creativity.

<u>5</u> *Description* (1-5 points): A written description of the iteration rule used to generate the image has been provided. The description is clear and makes sense when viewing the fractal image.

<u>5</u> *Problem* (1-5 points): A problem has been provided that can be answered by using the fractal image. The question should be thought-provoking but practical, given the picture presented.

<u>5</u> *Solution* (1-5 points): The problem posed includes a clearly worked solution and is mathematically accurate.

<u>50</u> TOTAL SCORE out of 50 possible.

<u>100</u> PROJECT GRADE (= TOTAL X 2)

When students complete the Fractal Project, they share their work in small groups and turn them in for assessment. Note that the rubric provided gives the students very concrete directions and sets realistic expectations. Students were actually involved in the creation of this rubric, and their ownership directly flows from generating the benchmarks for success.

GRAPHING CALCULATOR PROGRAMING PROJECT — WRITING ALGORITHMS, LOGICAL THINKING AND REASONING, USING A GRAPHING CALCULATOR

Many students in many secondary and middle school classrooms actively use graphing calculators to explore mathematical concepts. Sometimes, teachers "teach" students how to write simple programs for the calculator, while other students explore and figure out how to do this on their own (or simply download programs that were created by someone else). If a teacher spends some time on utilizing the programable capabilities of the calculator, students can be required to write a program of their own, to suit their needs. The appropriate use of graphing calculators and interactive computer software supports the NCTM technology Principle in the *Principles and Standards for School Mathematics* document (2000). This project can be done individually or in pairs, and it challenges students to design their own graphing calculator programs and to prove that the programs work properly.

GRAPHING CALCULATOR PROGRAMING PROJECT

Rationale:

The purpose of this project is to assess (measure) your ability to write a program for your calculator and your sense of logic that is required to write such a program.

Requirements:

You are required to write a program for your graphing calculator that performs some mathematical calculation that is more easily done on a calculator than by hand. The mathematical content can vary — algebra, geometry, discrete mathematics, probability and statistics — you may choose from any area that you want. You are expected to do the following:

♦   Write the program and enter it into your calculator.

♦   Type up a "hard copy" of the program to hand in.

♦   Meet with the teacher for an interview during the week in which it is due to demonstrate what the program does and to verify that it works.

Due Date:

The "hard copy" of the program is due two weeks from today. Then, during that week, appointment times to demonstrate the program in an interview with the teacher will be assigned. Between now and then, you are free to ask questions of other classmates and/or run your ideas or drafts past the teacher for advice.

Grading and Criteria:

The grade on this project will count as one test score. The criteria for grading the project, as determined by our class, are as follows:

Rating Scale: + = Outstanding, ✓ = Acceptable, – = Needs Work

Rating Areas: The program will be rated in the following areas: (A) Uniqueness, (B) Level of Sophistication, (C) Whether It Works, (D) Usefulness, (E) Time Saving, and (F) Efficiency.

In the field test of this project, the teacher took the idea directly to the class and asked them for input on assessing their work. As the rubric reflects, the students devised the six categories for assessing the effectiveness of the program. At that point, the teacher took the criteria and designed a formal Assessment Form, onto which each student's scores were recorded after handing in his or her work.

GRAPHING CALCULATOR PROGRAMING PROJECT
ASSESSMENT FORM

Student Name: _____

Program Name: _____

A. *Uniqueness* — the program should be different and "clever" in what it does.

Score: _____   Comments:

B. *Level of Sophistication* — a program that is somewhat complicated is an indicator that the writer has a solid understanding of how to write logical programing steps. Also, the "Display" function should be used to provide the user with directions on what is being inputted, etc. Having an "Input" step also helps to make the program more general and more sophisticated.

Score: _____   Comments:

C. *Works* — the program should work, in all cases. Provisions should be made in the program for "special cases" that may cause it not to work at all times.

Score: _____   Comments:

D. *Usefulness* — the program should be useful toward your schoolwork. It should tie in with the content of classes you have taken this year or last year.

Score: _____   Comments:

E. *Time Saving* — the program should save the user a certain amount of work. A program, for example, that adds two numbers may work, but it would not really save a person any time and is fairly useless to have.

F. *Unnecessary Steps* — the program should be "efficient." The program should accomplish its task in as few steps as possible.

Score: _____   Comments:

If a teacher chooses to explore the programing features of a calculator, it can be difficult (if not, impossible) to generate a test that adequately measures students' ability to program. In fact, if the point of the unit or series of lessons is to teach the students how to write a program, then the assessment should reflect their ability to *write* a program, rather than to answer questions *about* programs. In that sense, this project is *authentic* in that it measures exactly what the teacher was trying to convey to the students in the first place.

Another feature that makes this project unique is that it involves an interview component. In order to accurately assess the usefulness and sophistication of the program, the teacher meets individually with each student. The student is to use the few minutes of the interview to demonstrate the program and show the teacher how it works. The teacher is then free to ask some follow-up questions or to test unusual cases to see how the student handled them in the program. For example, one teacher who used this project had an algebra student who wrote a program that found the equation of a line when two points on the line were entered into the calculator. During the interview, the teacher tested the points (–5, –3) and (–5, 7) knowing that the line would be vertical. When the calculator generated an error message, the teacher asked the student what had happened and then used the interview to discuss how the program could be "debugged" by adding a line that accounts for the case of a zero in the denominator. While a lengthy discussion on the use of interviews is beyond the scope of this book, interviews can be another powerful assessment alternative that allow the teacher to interact one-on-one with the student and ask follow-up questions.

There are many other examples of authentic, project-based assessments that a teacher can assign to students, either individually or in pairs or small groups. For example:

♦ After completing a unit on ratio and proportion, students can collect data at a local grocery store on the prices of various size containers of food and determine unit prices to write a report about what they found to be the "best buys."

♦ As part of a unit on fractions, students can be given copies of pages from a cookbook and asked to quarter, halve, double, and triple recipes that include fractions in the measurement of ingredients to produce a "new" cookbook that contains different serving sizes.

♦ When students are exploring area of circles and/or rectangles, they can contact local pizza establishments and compare the prices of a square inch of various sized pizzas to determine which size is the most economical (e.g., is it better to buy two medium pizzas or one large pizza? four medium pizzas or two extra large pizzas, etc.?). If each team of students is assigned a different restaurant, the class may be interested in team presentations to find the best buy in town.

♦ While studying probability, students can be asked to create a game that uses number cubes. They can be challenged to create two versions of the game — one that favors one player over the other and another that is a fair game.

♦ Students (or teams of students) can be given the name of a famous mathematician such as Descartes, Pythagoras, or Newton and be required to research the life and contributions of that mathematician. Then, students can either write a paper or present a dramatic skit to the class that teaches others about the individual.

- Students can be required to search the Internet for data that can be analyzed in a project. For example, students can research average temperatures or population changes for a particular city over a period of time and graph the data to make predictions about the future.

- Students can design the "ideal" bedroom layout, including a scale drawing of the floor plan and an estimate of the costs of furniture and materials to decorate the room.

- High school juniors and seniors are often heavily involved in selecting career areas. Each student can choose a career interest, interview two professionals who currently work in that field, and write a research paper on the mathematics used in that career and what he or she learned about the job.

When you think about it, the topic of virtually any mathematical unit can be assessed through the use of some kind of project. The key is to consider the type of activity that would demonstrate the students' ability to *use* the mathematics in a meaningful manner. Many teachers find it useful to begin with one project per semester or per quarter. Students can be involved in the development of the criteria or scoring rubrics, and additional projects can be added later, as the teacher gains familiarity and confidence in using this strategy.

Throughout this section, we have talked about the importance of observing student behavior in the classroom, often including participation as one of the components in the assessment process. In the next section, we will look at the practicality of using observations and generating checklists for use in the mathematics classroom.

Sample Observation Tips and Checklists

Mathematics teachers will often report that they use observation in their classes on a regular basis. This is probably true, since all teachers use at least some type of informal observational strategies in their classes to decide whether students are understanding what they are trying to teach. However, relatively few mathematics teachers report having objective, concrete strategies for observing and reporting student work in the classroom. The purpose of this section is to provide a few hints and examples to assist you in more carefully capturing student performance during class time.

The first general principle in making effective and accurate observations is to have a method for collecting the data. Often, we get to the end of the school day, and all of the classes seem to "run together" — it becomes difficult to sort out one student response from another. We need an easy but efficient way of collecting data on student performances. Probably the simplest method is to use mailing labels or post-it notes, as mentioned in Chapter 2. Write a student's name at the top of each sheet of paper, 3-hole punch the papers, and put them in a binder with sections for each class you teach. Then, have a set of mailing labels attached to a clipboard, and as students work, make simple notes about their performance, such as:

Heather — 12/16 — knew difference between acute and obtuse triangles

Daniel — 2/19 — only person at the table who remembered Pythagorean Theorem from last year

Megan — 4/12 — nice job assisting other students on the Checkerboard Problem (helped them find the formula)

Notice how each mailing label note includes the name of the student, the date on which it was recorded, and a short statement of student behavior. At the end of the school day, the teacher can peel the labels from the clipboard and stick them on the individual student pages in the binder. Of course, every student will not receive a comment every day, but the labels provide the teacher with an ongoing record of student performance. These labels, then, become particularly useful for Parent-Teacher conferences because they serve as specific indicators of performance on particular days. Other teachers make use of post-it notes by writing the comments on the notes and sticking them to the students' desks as they work. That way, students themselves have immediate feedback on what the teacher noticed. Then, at the end of the class period, the notes can be collected and placed on student pages in the binder.

A second guiding principle of conducting formal observations of students is to define the criteria for expected student behavior. Observing a class is much easier (and more effective) if the teacher and the students know what the teacher is "looking for." So, just as teachers define objectives prior to teaching a unit on a particular topic, there is a need to write down some specific features of classroom behavior that are anticipated and expected. For example, suppose that the emphasis in the mathematics classroom is going to be on the five process Standards — Problem Solving, Reasoning and Proof, Communication, Connections, and Representation. You may choose to have a sheet with student names and the Standards onto which notes can be made during class time which serve as evidence of student ability to use the process. An example is illustrated in Figure 3.6.

As the teacher walks around the room, anytime that a student exhibits a behavior that reflects (positively or negatively) one of the process Standards, the teacher can

FIGURE 3.6. SAMPLE OBSERVATION SHEET

Name	Problem Solving	Reasoning and Proof	Communication	Connections	Representation
Student #1					
Student #2					
Student #3					
Student #4					

record a brief note about the situation in the box. Communicating the contents of this chart to students in advance can help clarify the expectation that students should exhibit mathematical thinking. The major drawback, however, to both the use of mailing labels and a chart is that it can be time-consuming to write down even short phrases on a form. Consequently, teachers can make the process more time-efficient by specifying details of expected behaviors and generating a checksheet for observation. A checksheet does not require statements to be written, unless the teacher includes an optional "comments" section. Instead, the teacher can merely check a box or give a rating in a particular area when conducting observations. The method cuts back on paperwork and allows more students to be observed in a given class period. Again, the teacher should begin by making a list of all of the behaviors that are expected in the classroom during the observation. Suppose, for example, that the teacher is observing students working in pairs on the Graphing Calculator Programing Project described earlier in this chapter. The teacher could make a list and generate an observation form such as shown on the following page:

**OBSERVATION FORM —
GRAPHING CALCULATOR PROGRAMING PROJECT**

Name: _____

	Low	Ave.	High
Communicates effectively with partner	___	___	___
Able to properly use programing mode	___	___	___
Understands mathematical concept programed	___	___	___
Uses time efficiently	___	___	___
Helps partner when assistance is needed	___	___	___
Asks for help when confused	___	___	___

Comments:

Notice that the form is very direct in the six behaviors that the teacher will observe. And, while the teacher *could* observe whether the student takes notes while working or stays on-task throughout the class period, those skills were not listed on the form because they were not seen as a priority in terms of what the teacher values during this project. In short, the form should be specific and concise enough to make it usable. A form with 25 expected behaviors may appear comprehensive but will most likely prove to be unrealistic in a classroom setting with 20 to 30 students. The form, however, does include a "comments" section so that the teacher has the option to make additional notes, if necessary or desired.

Another teacher noticed that students in a middle school class were not listening to statements made by the teacher and other students. The students frequently asked the same question repeatedly during a class period and had a tendency to ask non-mathematical, technical questions that got in the way of advancing meaningful mathematical discourse. As a result, the teacher chose to implement an observational strategy that would impact student grades. On the following page is the form that was distributed to the students:

OBSERVATION OF CLASSROOM QUESTIONS

Rationale:

In the First Quarter, there were few students who consistently asked "good" <u>mathematical</u> questions. Good questions are those that follow up an idea by asking "what would happen if . . ." or a reflection that "I tried . . . but I can't figure out why . . ." These are the type of questions that keep a class flowing and make it interesting as students contribute to discussions. These questions should not be confused with routine, non-mathematical questions, such as "Should we write the date on the paper?" that do not promote classroom conversations.

Furthermore, there were far too many repeated questions (e.g., one person asks if the assignment has to be done on looseleaf, and ten minutes later, someone else raises a hand and asks exactly the same question). These type of questions indicate that (1) there is more interest in the classroom in "doing what the teacher asks" than learning mathematics, which is disturbing. Also, (2) it shows that many people are not listening to others, so they repeat questions.

Assessment Procedure:

The following assessment process will be used this grading period:

♦ 25 points (one-fourth the weight of a test score) will be based on Question-Asking

♦ Each person will begin the quarter with an *automatic 20 points*.

♦ Each time someone asks a "good" mathematical question that significantly contributes to a class discussion, that person will receive 1 point.

♦ Each time someone asks a question that is a repeat of an issue already discussed and resolved by the class, that person will have 2 points <u>deducted</u> from his/her point total.

♦ A person can earn up to 30 points for the quarter, meaning that a person asking at least 10 good questions can earn 5 bonus points for the quarter.

Every attempt will be made to ensure that each person has a fair chance of making contributions to class discussions so that one person does not dominate conversations (each of you needs to be fair to one another in this area as well).

In this case, the teacher was trying to promote the asking of "good" mathematical questions that enhanced classroom discourse, while also trying to eliminate repetitive questions that were not necessary. The teacher kept a spreadsheet grid on the desk with the names of the students in the left-hand column and several squares to the right of each name. A quick recording of "+1" or "-2" was made in the boxes when students asked questions. Also, if the teacher determined that the question did not advance the discourse but was also not repetitive, then the student received no points or deductions at all. In this way, the strategy and checklist were used to reinforce students for following a discussion and developing curiosity.

When we view an observational strategy or a checklist as a concrete listing of behaviors, it's really not that difficult to produce. The students can be involved in the list writing as well. If a teacher says, "Over the next few days, I'm going to watch you work and observe what you do," then students can be asked, "what kind of behaviors do you think I should look for?" Students can generate the descriptors which, then, become part of the recording form. The form, in turn, can focus its benchmarks on behavior (e.g., Is the student on task? Does the student listen well? Can the student function in a team setting?); on the mathematics (e.g., Is the student able to simplify a fraction? Can the student solve a linear equation? Does the student recognize a geometric sequence?); on dispositions (e.g., Is the student a flexible thinker? Does the student display confidence? Is the student interested in and curious about mathematical issues?); or some combination of these. Again, it is the priorities and values of the teacher and the course of study that will dictate the contents of observations and checklists.

The final principle we will discuss here is the issue of whether to include the observational data in the students' grades. Teachers and their students often have the idea that "if it's important enough to measure, then it should be included as part of the grade." However, this may not always be the case. As was discussed in Chapter 1, there are a variety of possible uses for assessment data. This issue will be explored further in the next chapter, but the point to keep in mind is that if we are looking for evidence that students are learning or that our teaching is having the desired impact, we may choose to use an assessment strategy such as observation to simply collect data to assess our own work. Instead of looking at assessment as a process of determining grades, we switch the focus to assessment for improving the teaching and learning process. The observational notes in our binder might simply help us get to know our students better, track their progress, and provide evidence for conversations with parents, counselors, and administrators, rather than quantifying them to determine final grades. In the case of the projects described in this chapter, it is possible that observation can have an effect on a project grade, but it is not necessary for every observational note to have an impact on grades.

CONCLUSION

A man who purchased hearing aides when he was 65 years old commented on how loud the car engine sounded and remarked that it had been decades since he had heard the sound of an airplane flying over his house. It was only after obtaining a tool to assist with his hearing that he began to notice what most of us would consider "common" sounds. A middle school teacher in an inservice course viewed a videotape of her lesson and commented, "I had no idea the students were making mistakes measuring with their rulers right before my eyes because I was so caught up in the lesson that I wasn't watching what they were doing." Similarly, when mathematics teachers adopt new, innovative methods of assessing student work, they often remark that they notice things about their students that they had never seen before.

When students are challenged to write answers to open-ended questions, the teacher gains a window into student thinking that is very different from soliciting "correct answers" to specific questions. The use of journals can enhance the relationship between a teacher and a student and assist the teacher in understanding the student's viewpoints and thinking strategies. When students conduct and present short- or long-term projects, the teacher gets the opportunity to watch them function and apply mathematics to real-life problem situations. Finally, as students are observed carefully in class, through use of checklists or more open-ended formats, the teacher begins to look for behaviors that might not have been noticed without the tools. There is certainly "more than meets the eye" in the mathematics classroom, and these assessment strategies can assist the teacher in delving more deeply into student thinking and progress.

The purpose of this chapter was to present several concrete, classroom-tested ideas that can be used "as is" or as models as you consider adjusting and refining your classroom assessment processes. The four strategies detailed in this chapter — open-ended questions scored on rubrics, journals, projects, and observations with or without checklists — are the ones that many teachers cite as being the most practical to implement if they have historically used little more than tests, quizzes, and homework assignments to assess student progress. Any one or combination of these can serve as a starting point for reforming and rethinking your data-gathering processes. In Chapter 4, we will describe the various reasons *why* we assess student progress, and, as we alluded to in this chapter, the reasons transcend simply determining final grades. We will also answer the practical question of how to use project scores, rubric points, and observational notes to determine more "final" grades for students. The question about the relationship between assessment data and student grades is probably *the* most requested topic at teacher staff development projects focusing on assessment.

REFERENCES

Glasser, W. (1990). *The quality school: Managing students without coercion*. New York: Harper & Row.

National Council of Teachers of Mathematics. (2000). *Principles and standards for school mathematics*. Reston, VA: National Council of Teachers of Mathematics.

National Council of Teachers of Mathematics. (1995). *Assessment standards for school mathematics*. Reston, VA: National Council of Teachers of Mathematics.

4

DETERMINING FINAL GRADES

"Okay, I have collected all of the data, but how do I figure out their final grades?"

If you implement even a sampling of the suggestions for change that are presented in this book, you may find yourself overwhelmed with a great deal of data concerning your students' performance. In fact, many teachers, as they try to improve their assessment practices, find that they can get buried in binders of observation and interview notes, lists of rubric scores, and student project posters hung on the wall. And they can be almost paralyzed by the thought of using all of this information to determine grades for students in their classes.

Before getting overly preoccupied with calculating final grades, we need to accept the premise that the equation *assessment = grades* is false. Recalling the discussion from Chapter 1, assessment is an information-gathering process. While the data can eventually be used to determine final grades, not every piece of information collected during routine assessments needs to become part of a final evaluation or grade. In this chapter, we will begin by discussing the reasons for conducting assessments in the mathematics classroom. Then, we will look at specific ideas of how the combination of various assessments can be used to determine grades, as well as how the data can be used for several other purposes that transcend "grading."

WHY DO WE ASSESS STUDENT PROGRESS?

Student performance is assessed in mathematics for a number of reasons, and determining final grades is only one of them. In the *Assessment Standards for School Mathematics* (NCTM, 1995), the NCTM states that there are four purposes for conducting assessments:

- ◆ Monitoring student progress (to promote growth)
- ◆ Making instructional decisions (to improve instruction)
- ◆ Evaluating students' achievement (to recognize accomplishment)
- ◆ Evaluating programs (to modify a program)

The first of these purposes is the emphasis of some traditional assessments such as homework or quizzes — to set goals for students and then to determine the degree to which the students are accomplishing those goals (or "are meeting the outcomes") throughout the unit. As teachers, we want to know which of our students are progressing according to our expectations, which students need more of a challenge, and which students are in need of intervention. The second purpose — making instructional decisions — is important but often forgotten in the busy life of a teacher. Each day, students provide valuable feedback that can assist the teacher in making decisions that might affect the focus of the next day's lesson, the example used in class to make a point, the pace at which the class should move, and so forth. When we are blind to these cues from our students, we begin to "teach mathematics" instead of "teaching mathematics to adolescents," and these are very different aims. Assessment data gathered through informal means, such as observations and brief interviews with individual students, can be instrumental in guiding the flow of day-to-day instructional decisions.

The third purpose of assessment, as put forth by the NCTM, refers to the formal process of determining grades and reporting them so that the students and their parents are aware of whether the students have accomplished the intended goals and objectives over some period of time. In the eyes of many people — both educators and community members alike — this third statement is viewed as *the* purpose for conducting assessment. The final purpose is to make a decision on the effectiveness of an entire mathematics program. This purpose may result in building, district, or state level assessments being administered to measure progress.

In many states, some type of proficiency test or graduation examination has been established to ensure that teachers are addressing the intended outcomes from their courses of study, as well as to determine the degree to which students are mastering the intended outcomes. Similarly, many local school districts administer additional competency tests that measure the effectiveness of the local courses of study. The data from these standardized tests, in turn, can assist in determining whether the entire program is meeting its goals. Then, if the building, district, or state feels that a change in the program (which may include updated objectives, a change in textbook series, the implementation of an innovative instructional method, and the like) is necessary, modifications can be made.

Figure 4.1 is a visual display of the purposes of assessment, as outlined in the NCTM Standards document. Notice that different assessments can be conducted to accomplish the various purposes. For example, a final exam at the end of a quarter or semester in a middle or high school mathematics class might be an appropriate way of gathering data to meet the third purpose — evaluating achievement. However, this exam, like many chapter or unit tests, is "after the fact" and probably not very useful in a teacher's attempt to improve instructional practices along the way. Similarly, a reading of student journals can be very helpful in monitoring their progress over time but much less useful (if at all) in evaluating the effectiveness of a district's curriculum

FIGURE 4.1. THE FOUR PURPOSES FOR ASSESSMENT

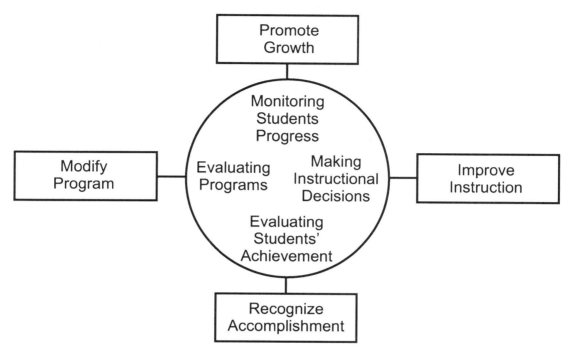

(Reprinted with permission from the *Assessment Standards for School Mathematics*, NCTM, 1995.)

or textbook series. Consequently, a teacher should not despair over the lack of ability to "use all of the collected data" in the process of determining final grades because evaluating achievement is only one of four reasons why these data are collected in the first place.

It is important to take the time to decide why one is conducting a particular assessment. All too often, a test is administered to a class not out of the desire to find out what the students know but in response to a perceived need to produce another score in the grade book before midterm! And while there is nothing inherently "wrong" with giving a written test, we shouldn't kid ourselves into believing that a student's score on the test will necessarily help us improve the quality of tomorrow's lesson or to get to know that student better as an individual learner. In short, the use of a variety of assessment strategies allows the teacher to gather data in different ways so that purposes beyond the evaluation of progress can be addressed. On the other hand, we have already discussed that students tend to take assessments more seriously when they "count for a grade" and that student accomplishments can be most accurately measured by using a variety of assessment strategies — looking at a series of pictures, rather than a single snapshot. If at the end of the quarter or semester, you decide to use the rubric scores, project grades, and journal entries together with your more traditional tests and quizzes, how can you use those numbers to determine the final grades? Let's look at a couple of examples that might help put the process of assessment into perspective.

ASSESSMENT AND FINAL GRADES

Suppose that you have historically relied entirely on the use of tests, quizzes, and homework scores to determine final grades. But after some reflection on your assessment practices, you have decided to include journal entries, projects, and weekly open-ended questions scored on a rubric as part of your grading scheme. Observation will also be part of the process but will be embedded in the projects and presentations completed by your students. You recognize that, by the end of the term, you will not only have a collection of scores on traditional tests and quizzes, but you will also have a list of rubric points and project evaluations to include in your grades. Now, you are faced with the task of putting all of the pieces together in a way that makes sense, is fair to the student, and is not overly time-consuming. Before implementing any innovative assessment ideas, you need to step back and think about how you will use those assessments to determine grades so that you are not faced with the arduous task of making sense of the data at the end of the grading period.

The first step in designing this assessment program is to determine the relative weighting of the various scores that will be recorded. Here is a list of the raw data that will be collected on each student:

♦ Test scores

♦ Quiz scores

♦ Homework scores

♦ Journal rubric scores

♦ Project grades

♦ Open-ended question rubric scores

It is entirely possible that one could weight the test average as 80% of the final grade. However, if the other five categories of assessment combine to make up only 20% of the grade, this scheme will send out a message to students that the other sources of data are not very important. Remember that the way a teacher weights the scores from various assessments will reflect the teacher's *values*. If students realize, for example, that their journals only "count" for 5% of their grade or will not count at all, then how likely are they to do their best work when composing a journal entry? A reasonable way to approach this process of weighting assessments is to make a list and then attach a percentage to each assessment category that reflects the value that you place on each of them. Of course, the total of the weightings has to be 100%.

Figure 4.2 serves as an example of how the assessments could be weighted. (Note that this table is *not* a recommendation of how they *should* necessarily be weighted but is simply used as an example to illustrate a point.)

FIGURE 4.2. RELATIVE WEIGHTING OF ASSESSMENTS

ASSESSMENT TYPE	WEIGHTING
Test Scores	35%
Quiz Scores	10%
Homework Scores	20%
Journal Rubric Scores	10%
Project Grades	15%
Open-Ended Question Rubric Scores	10%

In this case, the teacher has decided that tests and quizzes should account for less than half of the final grade for a student. A quick glance at the table also shows that tests only determine roughly one-third of the grade and that journal writing is valued equally with performance on quizzes and scores on open-ended questions. Students will inevitably notice the implications of these relative weightings of assessments and will respond accordingly. Once the relative weightings have been determined, then the next step of designing the method of assigning a grade in each area can begin. We will explore and describe each component of the student's grade.

TEST SCORES AND QUIZ SCORES

Test and quiz scores can be fairly easily "averaged" to determine the score in each of these areas. Teachers would simply use the same process they have used in the past for grading the papers and determining an arithmetic mean in each category. This process is the most traditional and probably the most familiar to teachers — the only difference might be that tests or quizzes include open-ended questions, in which case the teacher will need to decide how to use rubric scores as part of the test grade if the questions are to be scored with a standard rubric scale. Each open-ended question, for example, might simply be worth 5 points, where the number of points earned is equal to the rubric category into which the response falls (e.g., 3 points for a "3," etc.).

HOMEWORK SCORES

Homework assignments are graded differently by many teachers, depending on their personal style and past experience. For example, some teachers count all homework assignments as either "acceptable" (a score of 1) or "unacceptable/missing" (a score of 0). At the end of the grading period, if a student has 23 acceptable assignments out of 26, then the grade would be $\frac{23}{86} \approx 88\%$. Other teachers use the same policy but assign half credit for a paper that is submitted late or completed after the due date.

With a half credit policy, a student may earn, for example, $\frac{21.5}{26} \approx 83\%$ as a score in this area. Still other teachers score homework assignments on some type of a rubric. For example, a scoring scale might be as follows:

HOMEWORK GRADING RUBRIC

Your homework assignments will be scored by using the following scoring rubric:

2 = The homework assignment has been completed, turned in on time, and all errors have been corrected as the assignment was checked in class. All requirements have been met. The paper is neat and legible.

1 = The homework assignment is either (a) more than half completed but turned in on time, (b) completed but turned in a day late, or (c) completed on time but contains several errors that were not corrected in class. This paper is acceptable in that basic requirements have been met.

0 = The homework assignment is either (a) turned in on time or late but has less than half of the problems completed, or (b) has not been turned in at all. The paper is missing or unacceptable for credit.

Of course, when this teacher reaches the end of a grading period, the grade book will show a series of 0's, 1's, and 2's, instead of checkmarks to indicate completed assignments. How do these numbers translate to a grade in the homework area? First, we have to keep in mind that a rubric score of "1" using this scale *is acceptable*, as per the Homework Grading Rubric. Therefore, if the class had 26 assignments during a grading period, and a student scored a "1" on every assignment, that student would have accumulated 26 points. However, to call the student's grade for homework a $\frac{26}{50} = 50\%$ would be unfair because 50% is considered a failing mark in most schools, but the student has been told — by virtue of the rubric descriptors — that every homework assignment was acceptable! Consequently, the teacher needs a way to translate rubric points into percentages that are fair and make sense.

If we continue with this example, and the student has actually received 26 scores of "1" out of 26 assignments, then the teacher might conclude that the student has done C-work — acceptable but not good or excellent. So, we will assign a score of 80% to the student who earned 26 points since 80% in many school districts is an "average" C grade. Notice, however, that another student may have only completed 13 assignments the entire grading period — earning a "2" on all of them — skipped the other 13 assignments altogether, and will still earn an 80% homework grade. Is this fair? If not, then the teacher would need to modify the scale by adding a statement such as "a student can only earn a C or higher if more than half of the assignments have been at least acceptable" or some similar descriptor. To others, this might still seem fair, and no additional disclaimers would be necessary.

In the same class, if a student earns a "2" about half of the time and a "1" the other half of the time, then we might conclude that the student is doing B-work. Since, $(13 \times 2) + (13 \times 1) = 39$ the cutoff for a solid B might be a total of 39 rubric points. In many schools, a typical B would translate to about 88%. Of course, if the student scores a "2" on the majority of the assignments, an A would be a reasonable homework grade. This might be a student who earns, for example, a "2" on at least 20 assignments and a "1" on the others, so a minimum of $(20 \times 2) + (6 \times 1) = 46$ rubric points would be required for an average A of 96%. The logic here, of course, is to consider the expectations for the performance level required of a student to fall into each of the grade categories. After the major categories have been decided, then some interpolation can be used to define the rest of the scale. The result could be the sample scale shown in Figure 4.3.

In many schools, 70% is the lowest passing score. Therefore, if a student has at least acceptably completed half of the homework assignments, it may be reasonable to "pass" the student in the homework category by assigning a score of 70%, as shown in Figure 4-3. Notice that if a student earns at least 8 rubric points, the homework score is 60%, and we assume that any student earning less than 8 points is a special case that will require individual intervention. Or, the student might simply score a "0" for homework, as would be the case in any class where a student does not complete or hand in any of the given assignments.

Again, the sample in Figure 4.3 and the logic involved in setting it up are intended as guidelines and may or may not match your teaching style or comfort zone. You may choose to place several restrictions on how a student earns each grade, or you might want to be more lenient than this example, at least the first time you try this kind of grading scale. In fact, most teachers report that a conversion scale of this type is easiest to construct after having some experience on which to base the scale. For example, you might try this scale for one quarter and discover that some of your best students did not earn A's for homework because of a glitch in the system or because the scale was

FIGURE 4.3. SAMPLE CONVERSION SCALE FOR HOMEWORK RUBRICS TO PERCENTAGES

TOTAL RUBRIC POINTS (out of 52)	HOMEWORK GRADE
52 – 50	100%
49 – 46	96%
45 – 43	93%
42 – 39	88%
38 – 35	85%
34 – 31	82%
30 – 26	80%
25 – 21	77%
20 – 17	73%
16 – 12	70%
11 – 8	60%

not an accurate reflection of their performance. Due to experience, you gain a sense of how many rubric points are typically earned by students at various levels. Thus, the scale could be modified the next term (which will probably happen anyway because students are likely to have more or less than 26 assignments, prompting the creation of a modified conversion scale). The point here is that assessment, in general, should be viewed as being very malleable. We can go into a grading period with one idea, test it out, and drop, modify, or add to it in the following period. As with many endeavors in life, we learn by trying to do business differently and then reflecting on how it could have been done better, resulting in a continuous flow of change.

JOURNAL RUBRIC SCORES

As was discussed in Chapter 3, journals can be assessed in a variety of ways. As with homework assignments, some teachers simply score them as "complete" (a score of 1) or "incomplete" (a score of 0) each time they are collected and then assign a final grade based on the percentage of times that students earned a "complete" compared to the total number of times the journals were collected. So, if the teacher collected the journals about every two weeks — say, six times during a quarter — and a student had a "complete" journal 5 out of 6 times, the score would be $\frac{5}{6} \approx 83\%$ for the grading period. In this case, a "complete" journal would be one in which the student responded to all of the required prompts and provided a reasonable response for each of them. However, some teachers use a rubric that is similar to the Homework Grading Rubric described in the previous section. They might use this scale to differentiate between students who wrote entries that met the bare minimum requirements, versus those who exhibited significant mathematical problem-solving and reasoning skills. In this case, a method of converting the rubric scores to a percentage is often needed. Again, the teacher should begin by thinking about the number of rubric points that might be accumulated by a typical "A-student," "B-student," and so forth, and then build a conversion scale like the one presented in Figure 4.3 but adapt it to journal entry scores. In this way, the journal grade for a grading period can be reflected as a single percentage mark.

PROJECT GRADES

Project grades tend to be a little easier to average into a student's grades. As described in Chapter 3, an established rubric for a project can indicate levels of performance such that a percentage-type grade can be earned. Often, a teacher's observation of student work, or even the results of a brief interview with the student, can be factored in as part of the grade so that information on a checklist does not "stand alone" as an assessment grade per se. Therefore, any projects conducted during a grading period can be designed so that they result in a percentage score, and like tests or quizzes, the project grades can be averaged if there is more than one project in the period. Teachers need to decide, however, how heavily to weight any individual project. Some projects may carry the same weight as a test score (100 points), while others may be weighted as half of a test (50 points) or as a double test score (200 points). The decision on the weight of any individual project or presentation often depends on how much work is required by the student , the importance of the project's content, and the amount of time it takes to generate the product.

OPEN-ENDED QUESTION RUBRIC SCORES

The last assessment category for our example is the regular issuing and grading of open-ended or free-response questions. As was the case for both homework and journal entries, a method of converting rubric points to percentages is needed. Caution is advised here as decisions about these scales are made. Many educators, parents, and students make the mistake of viewing individual rubric scores on open-ended questions as a percentage or grade unto themselves, as was discussed in the Conclusion of the last chapter. Thus, if a student scores a 4 on a 5-point rubric, that student might view the grade as an 80% since "4 out of 5 points is 80%." But this is *not* the way that rubric scores were intended to be interpreted. The score of "4" is merely a comparison of the quality of the response to the standard that is established by the rubric. The numerical score is nothing more than a performance level indicator and should never be interpreted as the numerator of a rational number. Most would agree, in fact, that if a teacher utilized a 5-point rubric (six levels when 0 is included), a student who routinely scores a "4" is probably doing A or high-B level work. And, of course, A-B work is not characterized by a score of 80% in most school districts.

Using a 5-point scale for scoring open-ended questions on a rubric, the descriptive categories might be:

5 = Excellent

4 = Good

3 = Acceptable

2 = Fair

1 = Attempted/Needs Work

0 = No Attempt

In this light, we want to avoid the temptation to consider a score of a 5 as an "A," a 4 as a "B," and so forth, because again, an individual response to one question is difficult to assess as exhibiting the characteristics of an A-level performance. To look at a single student response to a question that is marked as a "4" and say that the student has earned a "B" would be similar to looking at the response to one question on a test and saying that if the student earned half of the credit on that one item, the conclusion is that the student is doing F-work (because of only earning 50% of the available points). Instead, the test is graded as a whole, where that one item is only one piece — maybe 5 – 10% — of a much larger puzzle. Similarly, a student response to one open-ended question needs to be considered in light of responses to several other questions over the course of the grading period.

Let's suppose that the students were asked to respond to two open-ended questions per week throughout the grading period, with each item scored on a 5-point rubric that was designed by the district. Over the course of nine weeks, the student has responded to 18 questions and could have earned up to $18 \times 5 = 90$ rubric points. On this scale, what type of "average" performance would equate to a final grade of an A? What about a B? Of course, the answers to these questions are going to vary, depending on the values of the teacher and experience with using open-ended questions as part of the grading scheme. It may be reasonable, for example, to assume that if a student routinely scores either a 4 or a 5 on the rubric, then the student is probably doing A-level work. Since $(9 \times 5) + (9 \times 4) = 81$, we might conclude that the cutoff for an A in this category is 81 points. Similarly, if a student generally earns a 4, with a score of 3 every now and then, we could say that this is a B-level performance. And since, for example, $(12 \times 4) + (6 \times 3) = 66$, we might make 66 points out of 90 as the cut-off for a B.

You might notice that $\frac{66}{90} \approx 73\%$, which is either a C or a D in most school districts, but again, this illustrates the major point here — the rubric scores are not intended to be used directly to determine percentages. The student who rarely seems to score higher than a "1" or a "2" (with a "0" and a "3" every now and then) will earn a total of about 25 rubric points for the grading period and probably deserves a D. And, perhaps, the band for possible scores that put a student in the C-range might be arguably larger than the band for the other grade levels.

With these guidelines in mind, we can interpolate the other grade conversions to complete this process. In this example, we will assume that the teacher creates only six performance levels for open-ended question responses — a perfect score, A, B, C, D, or U. An example of the conversion scale is presented in Figure 4.4.

FIGURE 4.4. SAMPLE CONVERSION SCALE FOR OPEN-ENDED RUBRICS TO PERCENTAGES

TOTAL RUBRIC POINTS (out of 90)	OPEN-ENDED QUESTION GRADE
90 - 86	100%
85 - 81	96%
80 – 66	88%
65 – 45	81%
44 – 25	73%
24 - 18	60%

The conversion scale in Figure 4.4 makes sense because if a student generally scores a "3" on the rubric, which is the Acceptable category, we would expect that individual to be a typical C-student. And, $18 \times 3 = 54$, so the student would earn around 50 points and be assigned an 81% (C). Similarly, if a student did nothing more than to attempt a problem each time but consistently scores a "1" with an occasional "0" or "2," then the student probably is not passing in the ability to write responses to open-ended questions. The score of 60% is appropriate, therefore, because it falls at or below the passing grade in most school districts. As was the case for the homework percentages, each teacher might determine slightly different cutoffs, and the table might change from one grading period to the next. As we gain experience with scoring papers on a rubric and tallying rubric points at the end of the term, we eventually create a system that makes sense to the teacher and the student and serves as a fair representation of student performance.

The Final Grade

At the end of the grading period, the final averages from each of the six assessment strategies can come together to determine the grade. An example of a student's calculated grade is presented in Figure 4.5.

FIGURE 4.5. DETERMINING A FINAL GRADE

ASSESSMENT TYPE	AVERAGE	WEIGHTING	POINTS EARNED
Test Scores	78	35%	$78 \times .35 = 27.3$
Quiz Scores	82	10%	$82 \times .10 = 8.2$
Homework Scores	85	20%	$85 \times .20 = 17.0$
Journal Rubric Scores	90	10%	$90 \times .10 = 9.0$
Project Grades	98	15%	$98 \times .15 = 14.7$
Open-Ended Question Rubric Scores	88	10%	$88 \times .10 = 8.8$
TOTAL		100%	85

The data in Figure 4.5 indicate that the student had a 78% test average and an 82% quiz average. When put together with an 85% for homework, a traditional grading scale would almost inevitably place the student in a C-level performance category. However, the power of using multiple assessment strategies shows that the tests, quizzes, and homework assignments do not constitute the total picture. In reality, the student was able to perform extremely well on a quarter-long project and maintained a very good mathematics journal. Although the student's performance on open-ended questions was not consistently strong, the other factors were able to propel the grade to 85% and earn the student a B –, rather than a C. On the other hand, we can all cite examples of students who tend to perform well on tests and quizzes but have difficulty communicating mathematical ideas and applying them to real-life problem-solving situations. The grades of these students may be negatively impacted by the use of multiple assessment strategies. Because of these types of students, it is not accurate to assume that using a variety of strategies tends to "water down" the grades or make it easier for students to earn A's and B's, a common criticism of the use of alternative assessments. In fact, in many cases, exactly the opposite is true.

Now, you may look at the data in the table and say, "I'm not sure that the student deserves a B due to the mediocre test performances." If so, then there are two possibilities (though one might imply the other): (a) you are still adhering to the "old rules" that say that test scores should dominate the decision on grade determination, or (b) you may not agree with the way that the various assessments were weighted in the first place. Perhaps you would feel more comfortable if the test average were weighted 45% instead of 35% or that homework would be 25% instead of 20%, and so forth. But these are decisions that each teacher must make on an individual basis, determined at least in part by the message that the teacher wishes to send out to students about what is valued in class. While the notion of eliminating tests altogether has not been entertained here, we could certainly make an argument for even lowering the test weighting to 30% and eliminating quizzes altogether, thus allowing journals, projects, and open-ended questions to weigh more heavily in the grades. The relevant questions, then, that each teacher must ask here are the following:

♦ What do I think is important (of value) in my classroom?

♦ Does my grading scale communicate what I value to my students?

♦ Am I confident that the final grades in my classroom are an accurate evaluation of each student's progress?

Assessment and final grading methods are inherently unique to each teacher. But the scenario described in this example was designed to show that there are alternatives to determining final grades based on tests, quizzes, and homework, which tend to dominate many mathematics classrooms today. The example also addresses the concern that teachers express when they realize that rubric points earned by a student are not intended to be used directly to compute percentages. You may come up with a different formula that works more effectively, but this example might be the engine that gets the individual thinking processes in motion. Finally, teachers need to realize that since assessment is conducted for a variety of reasons, not necessarily all data that are collected regarding student progress and performance will be used in determining final grades. Sometimes, we simply want to gather information on how students are thinking for the purpose of adjusting our lesson plan to fit their needs. We will address this issue in the next section.

ASSESSMENTS FOR OTHER PURPOSES

A study conducted by Miller (1992) showed that when algebra teachers began classes a couple of times a week by presenting their students with short writing prompts, they gained deeper insights into student thinking and were more likely to adjust lesson plans than when prompts were not issued. Interestingly, however, these prompts and short journal entries were not "taken for a grade." Instead, they were used as catalysts to spark the thinking of students, and the teacher would merely take a couple of minutes to leaf through the responses at the beginning of class to see if any modifications in the daily lesson plan would be necessary. While these journal entries did not affect student grades, they served as a very significant influence on the lesson the teacher was about to present. The message here is that not all assessments need to be employed in the process of determining final grades. In fact, data intended to assist in making instructional decisions or to evaluate a total program are generally not very useful for determining grades. Yet to ignore these assessments because they do not contribute to final grades would most likely be a mistake.

In Chapter 3, we discussed, for example, the use of mailing labels on which to record observational notes of student performances during instructional episodes. The open-ended nature of these notes allows the teacher to comment on the dispositions (attitudes) and the mathematical competence of students to help keep a running record of progress. Furthermore, these labels can be extremely useful at parent-teacher conferences, as a teacher can pull up a particular student's label page and describe specific classroom behaviors observed on given dates. However, if a teacher were to take these labels and attempt to use the information they contain to determine a grade in a class, the result would more than likely be total frustration. In short, the open-ended, mailing labels (or post-it notes) approach to recording student behaviors is not generally useful in the process of calculating final grades in a course. On the other hand, we cannot dismiss this assessment strategy on the grounds that it does not contribute numbers to the grade book. Instead, these records paint a picture of individual student progress that can shape the teacher's lesson planning process and assist in meeting each child's individual needs.

On a broader scale, examinations such as the PSAT, the ACT, the SAT, local competency tests, and state proficiency and graduation tests are not of much use in determining grades either. But these types of tests have the potential to provide valuable feedback on how students are performing "as a class," "as a district," and "within a state (province)." If, for example, proficiency test scores indicate a district-wide deficiency in demonstrating knowledge of geometric concepts, then the district can use the data to identify the weakness and develop a list of strategies to address the problem. The district might, for example, decide to realign or rewrite the local course of study; they might consider the adoption of a new textbook series, or they might plan a comprehensive staff development program to inservice teachers on the latest research on how adolescents learn geometry. Standardized tests are often viewed as political tools and a worthless waste of student (and teacher) time and energy. And while this opinion is probably true in many cases, we also have an excellent opportunity to capitalize on a mandatory testing program such that data gathered from the tests can serve a helpful purpose in the schools.

One of the assessment strategies that is not discussed at length in this book is the use of interviews with students. For example, teachers sometimes schedule formal, periodic, individual or group interviews with students, asking questions about current content under study. These interviews allow the teacher to ask follow-up questions, which is not possible with journal entries and many projects. In turn, systematic interviews often affect final grades, and many teachers are very skilled at this process.

A description of interviewing techniques in this book would need to be rather lengthy because the ability to interview a student effectively is an art that is developed with considerable practice.

However, many teachers do interviewing very well, at least on an informal level. They walk around the classroom and ask key questions to a sample of students as they work on a problem or engage in a discussion to get the "pulse" of the class. Similarly, when students are asked to go to the chalkboard to solve a problem and explain their reasoning, the teacher has a unique opportunity to probe their thought processes and look for misconceptions. And while informally interviewing students as they work alone, in teams, or at the chalkboard is an effective way to collect informal data on how students think about mathematics, the interviews rarely "count" toward grades. But like the mailing labels example, we don't want to throw out interviewing as an assessment strategy simply because it does not directly impact grades.

As teachers, we regularly and routinely assess our students' progress, both in terms of mathematical content and attitude development. Some of the assessments we conduct are rather formal — tests, quizzes, homework assignments, standardized tests, and even projects. Other assessments, by nature, tend to be more informal — journal writing, responding to open-ended prompts, and simple interviews. By using rubrics and conversion scales, even some of the informal strategies can be standardized and formalized and, therefore, contribute to final grades. The process of writing entries in a journal, which tends to be informal and idiosyncratic, can become a formal assessment strategy if the teacher is careful to define expectations and has a plan for implementing it.

CONCLUSION

As part of an activity designed to promote the topics of combinatorics and probability, Mr. McArthur posed the following problem to his mathematics class:

Take out a sheet of paper and number it from 1 to 5. I am going to give you a quick pop quiz that is True-False. (hesitates, looking confused and upset) Oh, no . . . I completely forgot to bring the questions with me. No problem . . . I just want you to guess the five answers. Do your best.

After the students had written their five responses on paper, Mr. McArthur proceeded to read the answer key to the students. "True, False, False, True, True." Then, he asked the students to raise their hands if they scored a 100%. In the class of 21 students, 4 of them had their hands raised. Mr. McArthur smiled and asked, "Should we have expected any more than four people to get 100% on this quiz? Or should the number of perfect scores have theoretically been less than that? How do you know?" The students went on to explore the problem and realized that since there were two possible answers to each question, there were $2^5 = 32$ possible answer keys. Therefore, in a class of 21 students, we would not have expected more than one person, if any, to have randomly guessed all of the answers correctly.

What is the significance of this story? This situation actually did recently occur in an eighth grade classroom, and the most interesting result was not how students went about solving the problem. Instead, it was the reaction the students had to the problem. As soon as Mr. McArthur hesitated and said that he had forgotten to bring the questions, the following queries were heard in the classroom:

- So, do we still have to take the quiz?

- Are you going to take this for a grade?

- Can we throw the quiz out if we don't do well on it?

- Are you serious? This could wreck my grade!

- Is this going to "count"?

In other words, students were almost incapable of participating in the mathematical activity itself because of their prevailing preoccupation with how the experience might affect their grades. The only way that he could respond and get on with the example was to ignore the questions and move forward, which he did.

If we tell our students that we will observe them working in teams during a project, their behaviors are most likely to be affected if we tell them that "25% of your grade on this project will result from those observations." Also, if we tell our students that we want them to write complete, thoughtful responses to prompts in their journals, the statement is made considerably stronger by explaining that they will be scored on a rubric that reflects higher grades for people who write thoughtful responses, rather than simplistic answers. If we can creatively devise ways to collect assessment data and transform it to "numbers" that can be used compatibly with a required local grading scale, then we have the potential to measure the progress and achievements of our students well beyond what is possible with pencil and paper, as was discussed in Chapter 1.

In this chapter, we have looked at the issue of converting rubric and other scores into percentages to assist teachers in managing grade books. Clearly, there are some strategies for assessment that lend themselves to being part of grade calculations, while others serve the broader purposes of assessing our own teaching and evaluating the effectiveness of an entire mathematics program. As you decide which assessment strategies to adopt for use in your classroom, keep in mind that you do not have to simply "add" techniques onto what you already do. Instead, it might be preferable to eliminate a strategy or two that you're currently using (or are planning to use) and replace them with different strategies that might provide a clearer window into student thinking. And, as was discussed in this chapter, the assessments that you choose and how you weight them in determining grades will send out a message to your students about what you value in the classroom. Ultimately, the selection of strategies and grading procedures is a function of what you believe it means to learn and teach mathematics.

Some teachers are already using a variety of assessment strategies and are looking for additional practical advice, while others are using fairly traditional assessments and are trying to determine a first step. Chapter 5 will explore the practical process of making change in the classroom. The final chapter is based on field-testing and suggestions made by nearly 250 teachers involved in an assessment project over a span of four years. It will provide some direction on how to take the details from Chapters 3 and 4 and put them into practice, taking into account the six assessment Standards which were suggested by the National Council of Teachers of Mathematics (1995).

REFERENCES

Miller, L.D. (1992). Teacher benefits from using impromptu writing prompts in algebra classes. *Journal for Research in Mathematics Education, 23* (4), 329-340.

National Council of Teachers of Mathematics. (1995). *Assessment standards for school mathematics*. Reston, VA: NCTM.

5

TAKING THE FIRST STEP

"I'm convinced that I need to rethink my assessment practices and have plenty of ideas on how to do it, but where do I start?"

Perhaps you had the experience of attending a workshop or hearing a keynote presentation that was so motivating that you couldn't wait to get back to your desk to try to implement the idea. However, reality began to set in as you realized the implications of change. You may have viewed the process of overhauling your assessment practices as more stressful than helpful, putting the idea to the side for "another day" because reorientation would be too difficult or time-consuming. And, you may have felt the same way as you read your way through this book.

Unfortunately, too many people "start" by trying to completely change everything that they do, rather than seeing professional development and growth as gradual processes. Many experts on change agree that as much as three to five years are generally necessary for a person or institution to significantly reorient their working behaviors. If you plan to change everything "overnight," you may be setting yourself up for failure — causing so much disappointment for not being able to meet all of your goals that you become paralyzed and don't change anything at all.

In this chapter, we will discuss the process of change itself, including the practical implications of implementing new assessment strategies in a classroom. To this end, we will begin by describing how to develop a reasonable and realistic assessment plan for a school year and then discuss how the NCTM assessment Standards can be used as benchmarks to measure the effectiveness of classroom assessment practices. Finally, we will reflect on how a teacher can measure the effectiveness of a new way of performing assessments in the classroom — ideas on how to assess the assessment plan. The contents of this chapter are based on several years' experience with about 250 teachers who underwent the process of change and then met in small groups to reflect on how they went about adopting new assessment strategies in their classrooms.

THE ASSESSMENT PLAN

As you reflect on the assessment practices that you currently embrace and compare them to the strategies presented in this book, you may be forming some ideas of how you can more accurately measure student progress and the effectiveness of your lessons. However, before moving forward into any type of implementation, it is crucial to consider your goals for making change and to avoid "biting off more than you can chew." In other words, it is important to devise a plan for changing your assessment practices that is realistic and attainable. Perhaps you have heard the expression that it is best to change in "baby steps" to avoid prematurely falling down. And, of course, an unrealistic plan will almost inevitably fail, convincing you that any attempt to change will fail, and this is simply not the case. So, plan to implement just one or two new strategies at a time, and — as was mentioned in Chapter 4 — whenever possible, let go of a current practice, rather than viewing new ideas as "add-ons" to what you already do.

In the assessment projects that led to this book, teacher-participants consistently thanked the instructional staff for encouraging them to "start small" so that they had enough time to develop confidence and familiarity with the use of rubrics and the like. In addition, teachers commented that the most valuable part of the process was actually putting a pencil to the paper to develop a written plan for changing assessment practices for the following academic year. A thoroughly developed plan is intended to serve as a road map to success as you reconsider your classroom practices. The assessment plan described here consists of three parts: (a) the rationale, (b) the general framework, and (c) specifics, such as tasks and rubrics you will use during the school year. We will now discuss each of the components of the plan.

RATIONALE

Every good plan or assignment should have a *rationale* underlying it. The rationale is the part of your plan in which you answer the question, "Why is it important for me to make a change from what I am already doing (or planning to do)?" To answer this question, you can begin by reflecting on what you are *already* doing in your classes and how the current features of your assessment program are falling short of where you believe they should be. For example, while reading the sections on journal writing in Chapter 3, you may have questioned the degree to which you really get to know your students as individuals during the school year. Perhaps you found yourself saying, "Yes, I'll bet there's a lot more to my students than is meeting my eye, and I need a better window into their thinking." If so, then you have at least one reason for change. Or you might have read the section on projects and presentations and realized that your students rarely, if ever, get an opportunity to connect the big ideas of mathematics in any significant way; thus, you have another reason to take a risk and change what you do. Remember that students, fellow teachers, administrators, and parents are all likely to ask you why you are conducting business differently than you did last year. And you need to have the confidence to state your rationale for change.

Also, as you think about the reasons for change, the rationale should help to identify those areas of assessment that need to be addressed and will, therefore, inherently suggest plans of action to overcome these weaknesses. For example, if you realize that open-ended questions are part of your state's proficiency testing program or your district's local competency test, you may also be aware that your students are not getting enough experience at writing responses to these types of questions. So, your rationale highlights the need for students to become better mathematical communicators, and, at the same time, the rationale statement will lead you to implement a system for including open-ended questions on a regular basis in your classroom. Keep in mind that we never want to "throw out the baby with the bath water," so many of the practices in which you already engage may very well be worth keeping. The key, of course, is to decide where the gaps are in your current assessment practices and to have the resolve to fill them with new and different assessments. Once you have stated a rationale for your change, which is fundamental to the process, it is time to sit down with a piece of paper and sketch out a general plan for how you will conduct assessment in the coming year. This general plan will be referred to as the *framework* for assessment. Lester and Lambdin (1996) provide an excellent description of how one might decide which assessment strategies to employ when developing an assessment plan:

> Clearly, the choice of evaluation techniques needs to be based on a multitude of factors, such as the type of mathematical skills to be assessed, the number of students to be evaluated, the amount of time available, the teacher's experience in teaching and evaluating higher-order thinking, the reason for the evaluation, and the availability of evaluation materials. The use of a variety of techniques permits a much more comprehensive evaluation of students. The choice of evaluation techniques will be quite personal, but in the end teachers need to choose techniques that are feasible for use in their particular classroom and that generate information appropriate for the goals of their own personal [assessment] plan.
> (NCTM, 1996, p. 7)

GENERAL FRAMEWORK

On a piece of paper, begin with a list of the assessment practices that you already employ in your classes and the weight that you give to each strategy. Let's say, for example, that a teacher's list includes the following:

- ◆ Tests (70% of the final grade)
- ◆ Homework Assignments (20% of the final grade)
- ◆ Classroom Participation Points (10% of the final grade)

This list should then be compared with the rationale for change that was constructed in the first step. Suppose, for example, the rationale states that, under the current procedures, students are not gaining enough experience with solving real-life problems over a period of time. Instead, the current structure only provides them with an opportunity to respond to relatively short questions during frequent, 45-minute testing times. As a result, the rationale for change includes a statement that students need to be engaging in one or two projects per grading period for the experience of applying their mathematical knowledge to realistic situations.

At this point, the teacher would take the current list of assessments and add "Projects" to it as a fourth item. In its draft form, the new list might look like this:

- Tests (60% of the final grade?)
- Homework Assignments (15% of the final grade?)
- Classroom Participation Points (15% of the final grade?)
- Projects (10%?)

However, upon looking at the list, it may become apparent that if students are going to be regularly engaged in some in-class projects, the teacher will be able to observe their ability to work together and their willingness to participate in classroom discussions in the context of the projects. Consequently, it might make sense to delete the Classroom Participation Points assessment strategy, rather than duplicating efforts and generating unnecessary grading work. Of course, once this item has been taken off the list, the teacher needs to revisit the message that students will be getting from the assessment plan to decide how the "extra" percentage points should be weighted. In its final draft form, the list might be:

- Tests (55% of the final grade)
- Homework Assignments (20% of the final grade)
- Projects/Observations (25% of the final grade)

As we discussed in Chapter 4, you may or may not agree philosophically with this framework for assessment, but it is intended as an example. In the end, each teacher must decide what is most important to measure, how to measure it, and how much each assessment should be relatively weighted. It may also be that, in the first year of change, the teacher will decide to keep Classroom Participation as one of the grading components. Finally, the teacher might maintain Classroom Participation notes throughout the year but decide not to count them toward the final grades, except as they apply to the rubric for a team project that is conducted in class. At mid-year or in the following school year, the strategy could be dropped if it is determined that Classroom Participation as a stand-alone strategy did not significantly contribute to assessment of the whole person. "More assessment" is not always equivalent to "better assessment"; instead, we try to keep a manageable number of assessments to use so that the teacher's workload is not unreasonably large, while still gathering enough data to inform the teacher and draw reasonable conclusions about student progress.

In the framework, the last issue is to specify the frequency and duration of each of the assessments for the school year. In this scenario the teacher may decide to administer five, one-period, written tests, two projects (one individual project and one team project), and four homework assignments per week for each grading period. The framework, then, is specific to the point of stating exactly which assessments will be used, how they will be used, and how they will be weighted in determining final grades.

SPECIFICS (TASKS, RUBRICS)

Once you have developed a rationale for making a change and supported the rationale with a general framework of which assessments you intend to implement, along with their frequency and weighting, the final step is to generate the details — the specific tasks and rubrics to use for the school year. The depth and content of this part of the plan will vary considerably, depending on the degree to which you are choosing to restructure your classroom assessment ideas. A teacher, for example, who is going to add projects but keep everything else the same (except for the relative weighting of assessments) may need to detail nothing more than four, quarterly projects that are intended for the coming year. However, this detail needs to include descriptions of the tasks, their placement in the context of the school year, and rubrics for scoring the projects when they are collected. On the other hand, another teacher who plans to implement biweekly open-ended questions will need to generate a list of as many of 75–100 questions that could be used throughout the year, carefully keyed to the outcomes for each unit as the questions are assigned. In addition, a "first cut" at a scoring rubric for assessing open-ended questions will need to be drafted. Often, a local school district already has its own generalized rubric for mathematics that can simply be inserted into the plan or, at most, modified to meet the needs of the teacher.

Teachers who are relatively new to using authentic assessments should be careful to create specifics that are detailed enough to be useful but not so overly rigid that they cannot be adapted and changed as time goes on. For example, one teacher in an assessment project began the school year with a binder filled with an entire school year's worth of carefully selected, open-ended questions and journal prompts. Despite hours and hours of research to gather and organize these questions, the teacher decided to incorporate the open-ended questions into journal entries and ended up failing to use most of the intended open-ended questions. The time spent assembling these questions, of course, was not entirely "wasted," but it might have been more realistic for the teacher to have written the specifics for the first grading period and include a simple outline of ideas for the rest of the year, thus leaving room for making adjustments while testing uncharted waters of assessment.

Finally, we have emphasized that students themselves should be involved in developing rubrics with which to score their work. If a well-intended planner writes all of the rubrics in detail prior to the beginning of the school year, there will be little room for students to take any ownership of the scoring benchmarks as projects and other tasks are assigned. Some teachers in the assessment project devised rubrics in advance but never gave them to students or even told the students that the rubrics existed. Instead, students developed "their own" scoring rubrics, with the teacher simply using the pre-planned rubric as an "answer key" to make sure that students had, in fact, included all of the major performance indicators that the teacher had anticipated. After all, students don't need to know that you have already established parameters for a rubric before asking for their input. On the other hand, some teachers present a "straw person" rubric to a class — a starting point or draft from which students can add and delete ideas until they mold and shape the rubric into their own model.

As you go through the process of writing a rationale for change, developing a general framework for assessment, and detailing the specifics for the school year, you will want to keep asking the question, "Is this a good assessment plan?" Of course, no one can tell you (except for experience itself, sometimes) what a *good* assessment plan looks like, since each is written by an individual to meet personal and professional goals. However, when the National Council of Teachers of Mathematics released *Assessment Standards for School Mathematics* in 1995, the Standards provided six benchmarks that a teacher can use to measure the viability of a proposed assessment plan. The assessment Standards themselves are, therefore, very important in the planning process and will be described in this context in the next section.

THE NCTM ASSESSMENT STANDARDS AS BENCHMARKS

The NCTM released the assessment Standards document in 1995 and then refined some of the thinking about assessment in *Principles and Standards for School Mathematics* (2000) five years later. The six Standards presented in the 1995 document are intended to assist educators as they attempt "to create a high-quality assessment process" (NCTM, p. 9). These six statements are the benchmarks with which one can determine whether an intended assessment plan makes sense and is likely to be effective and comprehensive. Interestingly, the authors of the NCTM document state that these same six benchmarks can be applied at the classroom, building, district, state, or even national levels. Hence, if an entire district were to consider restructuring its assessment processes, these Standards could be used to judge the new process, while at the same time, each teacher in the district could use them to measure classroom assessment effectiveness. We will briefly describe each of the Standards and their implications in writing an assessment plan.

THE MATHEMATICS STANDARD

Teachers should measure achievement by looking at how effectively students can perform on significant mathematical tasks. A significant task is perhaps the opposite of taking tests that are "trivial pursuits"; instead, the teacher is assessing important mathematical concepts and processes, such as problem solving, reasoning and proof, communicating, connecting, and representing. As a teacher develops an assessment plan, the document should be reviewed to ensure that proposed tasks for the school year (such as projects or journal prompts) emphasize mathematics that is significant and relevant to students.

THE LEARNING STANDARD

This Standard is a reminder that one of the aims of assessment is to promote learning in our students. Assessments should mirror the type of instruction that students are receiving in the classroom, and these assessments should "contribute to each student's learning of mathematics" (NCTM, 1995, p. 14). If the only purpose for including an assessment strategy is to collect data, and students are not likely to learn from the assessment process itself, then we need to consider dropping it from the list of strategies in the general framework. Assessment should enhance the learning process and be a natural part of our classroom, as opposed to viewing it as an end-of-the-unit "add on."

THE EQUITY STANDARD

Equity in mathematics and science education is perhaps the "hottest" topic among educators today. In a mathematics program with high expectations for all students, we need to realize that not all students think alike and that some students perform better on a particular type of assessment than other students. Therefore, the use of alternate methods of assessing achievement is important, as all students should have the opportunity to show that they have developed their mathematical knowledge. Some adolescents are effective test takers, while others are better at working in a team on a long-term project or writing a paper. The equity Standard reminds us that our assessment plan demands a mixture of various assessment tools so that each student has an opportunity to demonstrate mathematical competence.

THE OPENNESS STANDARD

Many of our students — and perhaps even you — have had the experience of getting an assignment back and not understanding what the grade meant or how it was determined. As we require students to make journal entries, to write responses to open-ended questions, and to make class project presentations, we need to be clear in our expectations and communicate to students and their parents the criteria by which their work will be judged. Many teachers address this Standard by distributing copies of rubrics prior to assigning work, by involving students in designing the rubrics, and by sending letters home to parents to explain the assessment process in the class. We need to be proactive in clearly stating, up front, what we value in the classroom. Assessment should never be a guessing game in which students try to guess what the teacher is looking for in an assignment or how grades will be determined.

THE INFERENCES STANDARD

When a student earns a B in your class, how certain are you that the student really deserves a B? The final grade in the course is *inferred*, based on the collection and analysis of assessment data. By ensuring that assessments match classroom learning experiences (which the 1989 NCTM evaluation Standards referred to as *alignment*) and that students are offered a variety of ways to demonstrate competence, we maximize the chances that our evaluations of their progress are accurate. As you examine the list of intended assessment strategies, ask yourself, "Will the evidence I collect give me a realistic picture of each student's achievement?" and "Am I confident that all of my A-students really deserve an A (that B-students deserve a B, and so forth)?"

THE COHERENCE STANDARD

The final Standard is really a summary of the rest and implies the degree to which all of the pieces that make up the assessment plan fit together and achieve the purpose for which the plan is intended. Assessment should match instruction and be seen by the student as a routine part of the classroom experience. Assessment, according to the authors of the Standards (1995) should "match the curriculum and instructional practice" and "inform teachers as they make curriculum decisions and determine their instructional practices" (NCTM, p. 22). This is the stage in which the teacher should look over all of the components of the assessment plan — the rationale, the general framework, and the specifics — and determine whether the entire plan "fits together" and makes sense. If so, we can say that the plan is coherent. Here is a summary of the six assessment Standards, in the language of the source document:

THE NCTM MATHEMATICS ASSESSMENT STANDARDS

Standard 1: The Mathematics Standard	Assessment should reflect the mathematics that all students need to know and be able to do.
Standard 2: The Learning Standard	Assessment should enhance mathematics learning.
Standard 3: The Equity Standard	Assessment should promote equity.
Standard 4: The Openness Standard	Assessment should be an open process.
Standard 5: The Inferences Standard	Assessment should promote valid inferences about mathematics learning.
Standard 6: The Coherence Standard	Assessment should be a coherent process.

(NCTM, 1995, pp. 11, 13, 15, 17, 19, 21)

As you complete your assessment planning process for a school year (or grading period), it is helpful to subject the plan to these six Standards to determine its overall adherence to the benchmarks. Ideally, you should be able to defend your assessment strategies by describing how the plan meets the expectations of each of the Standards. The Standards can be used both in the writing process and in the final stages, as you look back to decide if the plan makes sense. The assessment Principle from *Principles and Standards for School Mathematics* (2000) concludes by stating the following: "Teachers must understand their mathematical goals deeply, they must understand how their students may be thinking about mathematics, they must have a good grasp of possible means of assessing students' knowledge, and they must be skilled in interpreting assessment information from multiple sources" (NCTM, p. 24). These issues are all addressed in a well-developed assessment plan. And just as a lesson without a plan and a trip taken without a road map are bound for disaster, so is the teacher who tries to adopt new assessment ideas without clearly stating, detailing, and defending them in advance of their implementation.

Of course, if you construct a plan for change, the first grading period or academic year will tell much more of the tale of whether your plan was as effective as you had hoped. There is really no way to know exactly how the plan will work in the field without trying it, reflecting on the results, and refining your practices the next time. And, of course, every class and every year is different. An assessment plan that works with this year's students may or may not work next year; therefore, flexibility and ongoing reflection are imperative when adopting new assessment ideas. Teachers, however, often raise the question, "How will I know if my assessment plan actually worked?" This is a rather difficult question because there are many indicators that one can use to assess an assessment plan's effectiveness. Let's explore this issue by considering a case study of a high school teacher undergoing the change process in her mathematics classroom.

ASSESSING YOUR ASSESSMENT PLAN

Holly Joyce was a teacher at a suburban high school in the Midwest and was involved in one of the assessment projects for teachers. After reviewing her assessment practices, in light of available alternatives, she decided that it was time for a change in her classroom. Her current system of weekly tests and collecting mathematics notebooks was simply not providing her with an adequate picture of her students' achievement. She became interested in her students' ability to problem-solve and to communicate mathematically. So, she devised an assessment plan that included a rationale for growth and a framework that included journals, the use of rubrics for scoring open-ended questions, and two mathematics projects per grading period. She chose not to drop any of her current practices, as she feared that she would lose valuable data about her students on which she had relied for determining final grades in the past.

In the first month of the school year, reality caught up to Ms. Joyce. She found herself buried in 150 journals, 150 notebooks, 150 weekly tests, and the assessment of 300 individual projects for the grading period. In addition to administering open-ended questions and giving tests, she very quickly discovered that her assessment plan was unrealistic. While it appeared to be comprehensive "on paper" and met the guidelines established by the assessment Standards, the plan was failing for her. As a result, she decided to eliminate journal writing as a class requirement and cut the projects back to one per grading period. She continued to give her students open-ended questions but also cut back on the frequency with which she administered these questions. By the end of the school year, she felt comfortable with what she had done. She was disappointed that her plan had to undergo such a major revision, but she felt as though she got to see a side of her students that she had never experienced in the past — the process of watching them gather data and present long-term project reports. She once commented, "I was amazed at what my students could do in those projects. I kept thinking to myself that either the students this year were considerably more intelligent than in years past or that they've been able to do this level of work all along — the difference is that I had never *asked* them to do this kind of thing in the past. I guess that my students will only perform at the level I require. And my expectations have definitely raised the bar this year."

In her second year, Holly Joyce decided to reconstruct her assessment plan based on her experience. As she looked over the results of her first year, she realized that the mathematics notebooks that she had been collecting for several years of her career were not contributing anything to the picture of each student's progress that she had not seen through other assessments. Since they did homework assignments as part of their notebook requirement, she decided to have the students do their homework on loose leaf paper instead. That way, she could collect it daily, check it into a grade book, and hand it back so that she would not have piles of notebooks sitting around her room. She also revised her system of journal writing so that students would write three times a week, rather than every day, and she was able to reduce the number of times the journals needed to be collected, thus making it possible to put journals back into her plan. Thus, the second year featured traditional testing along with regular (but not daily) journal writing, open-ended questions, and one project per grading period. This second year went much more smoothly because she was familiar with the use of the rubric for open-ended questions and had already devised the projects and their rubrics from the following year. No modifications to the system were made during the course of the second academic year.

Upon reflection at the end of the second school year, Ms. Joyce decided that her students were still not being asked to do enough verbal communication of mathematical ideas — her journals and projects had emphasized only *written* communication. She also realized that at parent-teacher conferences, she had little to show the parents because the students had only completed one project and kept their journals and returned papers. So, in her planning for the third year, Holly Joyce began by designing a straightforward, four-level rubric for students explaining problems at the board, as follows:

PROBLEM PRESENTATION RUBRIC

By using index cards to make the process random, I will be asking you routinely to come to the board to explain homework problems to the rest of the class. Whenever you present a solution to the class, I will record a score for your presentation, as follows:

3 = The presentation of the solution and the way that the problem was solved were clear. Questions asked by the class were answered accurately. Confidence and an excellent ability to communicate mathematically were evident.

2 = The presentation included a correct solution, although the explanation of how the problem was solved was not clear. OR the explanation was accurate and clear, but there was an error in the solution itself that the class had to correct. Most questions asked by the class were accurately answered. Some confidence and an acceptable ability to communicate mathematically were evident.

1 = The presentation was not clear in that the solution had errors, and the class was unable to follow the reasoning. Questions raised by the class were not acceptably answered. Very little confidence was displayed, and the mathematical communication skills were lacking.

0 = Student refused to go to the board to attempt the problem.

Ms. Joyce decided to record these Problem Presentation Rubric scores in her grade book but not to use them in calculating grades for her students. Instead, she would periodically report the scores to the students and ask them to write journal entries in which they reflected on their ability to communicate verbally solutions to problems to the class. She thought that it would be helpful to have those scores available at parent-teacher conferences as a means of describing classroom behaviors of her students. She also decided to institute simple portfolios for her students in the third year. She would have her students maintain a portfolio of their work that would be collected once every grading period. The portfolio was to contain copies of three of their "favorite" journal entries, with explanations of why they chose those particular entries, graded tests with corrections of items missed, solutions to three samples of open-ended questions, and a summary of their grading period project and its assessment. At conferences, she would bring a crate of the portfolios along so that parents could see actual samples of their student's work as they discussed an individual's progress.

At the end of her third year of implementation, Ms. Joyce decided that it was time to step up the projects to two per grading period but to start to reduce her tests from weekly assessments to a test every two to three weeks. In her fourth year, she finally began to feel comfortable with the assessment plan, having gone through considerable revision and evolving from one that emphasized tests and homework done in notebooks to a plan that emphasized written and verbal communication of mathematics and real-life problem solving. Her assessments changed along with her values, and the strategies became more refined with experience.

The "case study" of Holly Joyce is presented here as a means to get us to think about the evolution of an assessment plan over time. Rarely does a teacher generate a plan that works, as proposed, in the first year such that it becomes *the* assessment process used by the individual for years to come. Instead, most people make a list of ideas they want to attempt, try them out for some period of time, and then improve upon the ideas over the years. In the case of Ms. Joyce, she took on more assessment ideas than she could handle in the first year (which is not unusual for teachers who become committed to making changes) and had to back off from the original plan and modify it each of the following three years. It was four years before she finally had her system down to an art, which is not to say it became a "rock" that can never be changed, but at least she had reached a happy medium between the data she wanted to collect and the methods that she felt comfortable with employing.

Notice that, each year, Ms. Joyce revisited the assessment plan and tried to decide whether it was actually being effective. While each person may develop a different way to determine whether the current assessment plan is working, several sources of data are available to make this evaluation. To determine the effectiveness of your assessment plan, you might:

♦ Reflect on the question, "Do I know each of my individual students better this year than I did last year?"

♦ Routinely ask your students to write journal entries in which they tell you whether they feel that the assessments you use in class give them the opportunity to adequately demonstrate their mathematical progress.

♦ Send a survey home to parents, describing the assessments you are using and asking them for any reactions or input, based on what their children tell them at home.

♦ Compare the academic progress of your students from one year to the next. If the plan is effective, then "getting to know" your students better should help you to be a better teacher, resulting in higher performance levels. Simply put, if the assessments are "working," then students should be developing mathematical competence better than they did last year. Can you prove that?

♦ Consider the amount of time you are spending on assessment, compared to the benefits derived from the changes. Is there a reasonable trade-off? Also, have the new assessments replaced former strategies, or have you continued to add ideas and made your professional life even more difficult in the process?

♦ Think about your assessment goals, as stated in your rationale. Decide whether the framework has any duplications of data that can be eliminated to cut down on your workload. (Notice how Holly Joyce dropped the mathematics notebooks and scaled back the number of journal entries because they did not appear to tell her anything more about her students than she already knew and were simply time-consuming.)

♦ Be sure to talk to colleagues in your building to compare and contrast various approaches to assessment. Feedback from other professionals, from the outside, can be a valuable experience as we sometimes become too engrossed in our own work to think about it objectively.

Of course, the overriding message here is that an assessment plan should be a living, changing, growing entity over time. Each year, a teacher needs to reconsider the rationale for the plan, determine a framework for action, and detail the specifics that will be needed to move forward on the new plan. But we have to accept the premise that nothing is perfect the first time we try it. We learn by making attempts, reflecting on our progress, and making refinements. The case of Holly Joyce can serve as a reminder that it's okay to make mistakes and that, like a fine piece of art made from clay, we can always go back and reshape it to make it better.

CONCLUSION

One of the recent trends in business and industry has been to adopt a slogan of "Ready? Fire! Aim!" This, of course, deviates from the traditional statement, "Ready? Aim! Fire!" because it emphasizes that, instead of sitting back and waiting until all of the conditions are perfect (which they never are), businesses need to get out and at least do *something* that can be refined later. Perhaps you remember waiting to buy a computer, recording device, or some other product, holding off until the latest technology had been released so that you were on the cutting edge. Of course, the myth is that if we wait "just six more months" the computer that we buy will be *the* state of the art for years to come. But the truth is that whatever computer we buy today will be obsolete in a couple of years. However, this should not keep us from buying a computer, for if we refuse to make the move, we find ourselves doing unnecessary work.

The analogy holds true for classroom assessment as well. If we choose to spend several years thinking about assessment, without actually doing anything about it, we will exhaust our energy on aiming and do little, if any, firing. Instead, if you feel that you are ready and motivated to make a change in the way you conduct assessment in your classroom, there is no better time than the present. Take a careful look at what you do, select one or two alternatives that sound interesting to you, and put them into practice. Like Holly Joyce, you are likely to find yourself "aiming" later, but it only becomes possible because you "fired" today.

In the end, the purpose of our role in the mathematics classroom is to develop our students into thinking, problem-solving individuals who possess the mathematical literacy to function effectively in our complex world. Because that world depends on people who are technologically literate and who possess the reasoning and communication skills to function on committees and working teams, our classrooms need to model real-world situations for middle and secondary school students. The traditional assessment procedures of giving tests and checking off homework assignments simply do not adequately measure students' ability to problem-solve, to reason, to communicate, to connect mathematical ideas to one another and to the real world, and to generate effective representations. The adoption of alternative methods of student assessment sends out a message to students, parents, and the community that there is more to mathematics than "right and wrong" answers. In turn, the assessment provides the teacher with valuable information that can be used in a variety of ways to enhance student achievement. And, in the end, it is raising the bar of expectations for *all* students that is the goal of our profession. Ultimately, a change in assessment practices should result in the enhancement of student achievement in mathematics.

In this final chapter, we have explored the very practical matter of taking a "first step" in changing assessment practices. A three-part method of designing an assessment plan for yourself was described (stating a Rationale, developing a Framework, and detailing the Specifics), as were the six NCTM assessment Standards (Mathematics, Learning, Equity, Openness, Inference, and Coherence) which can serve as benchmarks for measuring the potential strength of your plan. A case study of a high school teacher's experience with change and some concrete suggestions were provided to help you think about how to assess the effectiveness of your plan and to allow it to grow and change over time.

In the Appendix, you will find a list of print, video, and Internet resources that can be helpful in designing the details of your assessment plan. Remember that the object is to set yourself up for success, so it is generally better to begin with minor changes — "baby steps" — than to take on a long list of new ideas that are difficult to implement. Your students will learn about what you value in the mathematics classroom by virtue of the way that you assess their progress. If your students were asked today to write about what you believe is important in the mathematics classroom, what would they write? What do you *want* them to write? How can you change your assessment practices to bridge the difference between what they *see* and what you *want* them to see?

References

Lester, F.K. & Lambdin Kroll, D. (1996). In D.V. Lambdin, P.E. Kehle, & R.V. Preston (Eds.) *Emphasis on assessment: Readings from NCTM's school-based journals*, pp. 3-8. Reston, VA: NCTM.

National Council of Teachers of Mathematics. (2000). *Principles and standards for school mathematics*. Reston, VA: NCTM.

National Council of Teachers of Mathematics. (1995). *Assessment standards for school mathematics*. Reston, VA: NCTM.

National Council of Teachers of Mathematics. (1989). *Curriculum and evaluation standards for school mathematics*. Reston, VA: NCTM.

APPENDIX

Other Available Assessment Resource Materials

BOOKS

Barton, J., & Collins, A. (1997). *Portfolio assessment: A handbook for educators.* Menlo Park, CA: Addison-Wesley.

Barton, P. (Dir.). (1993). *Performance assessment sampler.* Princeton, NJ: Educational Testing Service.

Becker, J.P., & Shimada, S. (1997). *The open-ended approach: A new proposal for teaching mathematics.* Reston, VA: National Council of Teachers of Mathematics.

Beyer, A. (Proj. Coordinator). (1993). *Alternative assessment: Evaluating student performance in elementary mathematics.* Palo Alto, CA: Dale Seymour Publications.

Bright, G., & Joyner, J. (Eds.). (1998). *Classroom assessment in mathematics.* Lanham, MD: University Press of America.

Brutlag, D. (1994). *Equals investigations: Flea-sized surgeons.* Berkeley, CA: Lawrence Hall of Science University of California.

Brutlag, D. (1994). *Equals investigations: Growth patterns.* Berkeley, CA: Lawrence Hall of Science University of California.

Brutlag, D. (1994). *Equals investigations: Remote rulers.* Berkeley, CA: Lawrence Hall of Science University of California.

Brutlag, D. (1994). *Equals investigations: Scatter matters.* Berkeley, CA: Lawrence Hall of Science University of California.

Brutlag, D. (1994). *Equals investigations: Telling someone where to go.* Berkeley, CA: Lawrence Hall of Science University of California.

Bryant, D., & Driscoll, M. (1998). *Exploring classroom assessment in mathematics.* Reston, VA: National Council of Teacher of Mathematics.

Burton, G. (1993). *Number sense and operations.* Reston, VA: The National Council Of Teachers Of Mathematics.

California Assessment Program. (1998). *A question of thinking: A first look at students' performance on open-ended questions in mathematics.* Sacramento, CA: California State Department of Education.

Clarke, D. (1997). *Constructive assessment in mathematics.* Berkeley, CA: Key Curriculum.

Cross, M. (1995). *How to's in getting started with assessment & evaluation using portfolios.* Barrie, Ontario: Exclusive Educational Products.

Curcio, F., & Bezuk, N. (1994). *Understanding rational numbers and proportions.* Reston, VA: The National Council of Teachers of Mathematics.

Danielson, C. (1997). *A collection of performance tasks and rubrics: Middle school Mathematics.* Larchmont, NY: Eye On Education.

Danielson, C., & Marquez, E. (1998). *A collection of performance tasks and rubrics: High school mathematics.* Larchmont, NY: Eye On Education.

De Fina, A. A. (1992). *Portfolio assessment: Getting started.* New York: Scholastic.

Driscoll, M., & Bryant, D. (1998). *Learning about assessment, learning through assessment.* Washington, DC: National Academy Press.

Freedman, R. L. (1994). *Open-ended questioning: A handbook for educators.* Menlo Park, CA: Addison-Wesley.

Geddes, D. (1994). *Measurement in the middle grades.* Reston, VA: The National Council of Teachers of Mathematics.

Hart, D. (1994). *Authentic assessment: A handbook for educators.* Menlo Park, CA: Addison-Wesley.

Jasmine, J. (1994). *Middle school assessment.* Huntington Beach, CA: Teacher Created Materials.

Jasmine, J. (1995). *Portfolio planner: A step-by-step guide to portfolio assessment.* Huntington Beach, CA: Teacher Created Materials.

Kulm, G. (1990). *Assessing higher order thinking in mathematics.* Washington, DC: American Association for the Advancement of Science.

Lesh, R., & Lamon, S. J. (1992). *Assessment of authentic performance in school mathematics.* Washington, DC: American Association for the Advancement of Science.

Leutzinger, L. (Ed.). (1998). *Mathematics in the middle.* Reston, VA: The National Council of Teachers of Mathematics.

Moon, J., & Schulman, L. (1995). *Finding the connections: Linking assessment, instruction, and curriculum in elementary mathematics.* Portsmouth, NH: Heinemann.

Newman, V. (1994). *Math journal: Tools for authentic assessment.* San Leandro, CA: Teaching Resource Center.

Reys, B. (1991). *Developing number sense in the middle grades.* Reston, VA: The National Council of Teachers of Mathematics.

Ryan, C. D. (1994). *Authentic assessment.* Westminster, CA: Teacher Created Materials.

Schoenfeld, A. (Proj. Dir.). (1999). *Balanced assessment: Middle grades assessment.* (Package 1). White Plains, NY: Dale Seymour Publications.

Schoenfeld, A. (Proj. Dir.). (1999). *Balanced assessment: Middle grades assessment.* (Package 2). White Plains, NY: Dale Seymour Publications.

Schoenfeld, A. (Proj. Dir.). (1999). *Balanced assessment: High school assessment.* (Package 1). White Plains, NY: Dale Seymour Publications.

Schoenfeld, A. (Proj. Dir.). (1999). *Balanced assessment: High school assessment.* (Package 2). White Plains, NY: Dale Seymour Publications.

Schoenfeld, A. (Proj. Dir.). (1999). *Balanced assessment: Advanced high school assessment.* (Package 1). White Plains, NY: Dale Seymour Publications.

Schoenfeld, A. (Proj. Dir.). (1999). *Balanced assessment: Advanced high school assessment.* (Package 2). White Plains, NY: Dale Seymour Publications.

Seeley, A. E. (1994). *Portfolio assessment.* Westminster, CA: Teacher Created Materials.

Stenmark, J. K. (1989). *Assessment alternatives in mathematics.* Berkley, CA: Regents, University of California.

Stenmark, J. K. (1991). *Mathematics assessment: Myths, models, good questions, and practical suggestions.* Reston, VA: National Council of Teachers of Mathematics.

Vinton, L. (1994). *Math assessment grades 5-6.* Huntington Beach, CA: Teacher Created Materials.

Vogt, S. (1995). *Math journal writing and problem solving II: Grades 3-6.* Greensboro, NC: Carson-Dellosa Publishing Company.

Walen, S., & Hirstein, J. (1995). *Restructuring mathematics assessment: Suggestions from the classroom.* Needham, MA: Simon & Schuster Custom Publishing.

Westley, J. (1994). *Puddle questions grade 5: Assessing mathematics thinking.* Mountain View, CA: Creative Publications.

Westley, J. (1994). *Puddle questions grade 6: Assessing mathematics thinking.* Mountain View, CA: Creative Publications.

Westley, J. (1995). *Puddle questions grade 7: Assessing mathematical thinking.* Mountain View, CA: Creative Publications.

INTERNET RESOURCES

Brahier, D. J. (1999). Assessment Collaborative for Educators seeking New Directions. WWW document [www.bgsu.edu/colleges/edhd/programs/ASCEND].

Brahier, D. J. (1998). Assessment Project Involving Regional Educators. WWW document [www.bgsu.edu/colleges/edhd/programs/ASPIRE].

Brahier, D. J. (1997). Assessment Project Extended to the Northwest. WWW document [www.bgsu.edu/colleges/edhd/programs/ASPEN].

Brahier, D.J. (1996). Assessment Project for Erie County Teachers. WWW document [www.bgsu.edu/colleges/edhd/programs/ASPECT].

These sites include descriptions of each component for four years of a project on mathematics assessment for teachers of grades Pre-K-12. There are hundreds of assessment activities, which are grouped according to grade levels. These sites also give additional mathematics Web site links.

Champlin, C. (Dir.). (1997). MSD pike pathways to excellence training resources. WWW document [www.indianapolis.in.us/pike/training/pages/assess.htm]. (accessed 2/01)

This site provides links to several other resources on assessment, including links to NCTM, NSTA, SPA, and many more.

Daley, P., Diamond, M., Handy, S., & McKenzie, H. (1994). Authentic assessment in mathematics. WWW document [forum.swarthmore.edu/sum94/project2.html]. (accessed 2/01)

This page collects and organizes available Internet resources on Authentic Mathematics Assessment applicable to secondary schools.

Eash, D. (Proj. Dir.). Teacher/Pathfinder. WWW document [teacherpathfinder.org/School/math.html]. (accessed 2/01)

This page provides links to ideas for instruction and assessment in Algebra, Geometry, Probability, Statistics, and more.

Eisenhower National Clearinghouse for Mathematics and Science Education. New approaches to assessment on the Internet. WWW document [enc.org/classroom/focus/112345.nf_2345_38.htm]. (accessed 2/01)

This is located at the home of the Eisenhower National Clearinghouse. The site provides many Internet resources on assessment.

Eisenhower National Clearinghouse for Mathematics and Science Education. Toolkit for mathematics curriculum development. WWW document [http://watt.enc.org/online/ENC1665/1665.html]. (accessed 2/01)

This site features a Mathematics Toolkit designed by the Montana Office Of Public Instruction. One of the features of the toolkit is student assessment. Tasks, rubrics, journal prompts, and more are featured at the site.

Lasek, T. (Super.). (1999). Schools of California online resources for education: Assessment resources. WWW document [score.kings.k12.ca.us/assess.html].

Based in California, this site provides links to several other resources on the Web that support reform in mathematics assessment. (accessed 2/01)

Maryland Assessment Consortium. (1999). Mathematics assessment links. WWW document [http://mac.cl.k12.md.us:2000/links/AssessmentDBLinks/MathIndex. html]. (accessed 2/01)

Teachers are provided with a number of links to other Web sites that include helpful assessment ideas.

Maryland Assessment Consortium. Performance assessment resources in content area. WWW document [mac.cl.k12.md.us:2000/resources/content.html]. (accessed 2/01)

This site gives resources for teachers to use as ideas for assessment projects. The resources are for all grade levels and all subjects.

National Center for Education Statistics. National assessment for education progress. WWW document [http://nces.ed.gov/nationsreportcard/site/home.asp]. (accessed 2/01).

The home of The Nation's Report Card, this site contains a wealth of information on the NAEP test through the years, including sample items and performance trends.

Presson, A. Five tips for getting the best results from your school and students on the *high schools that work* assessment. WWW document [http://www.sreb.org/programs/hstw/assessment/5tips.asp]. (accessed 2/01)

This site provides teachers with five tips that will help their assessment go more smoothly in their classroom. This page also provides teachers with examples of open-ended questions to use in their high school classroom.

Queensland Association of Mathematics Teachers. (1998). Secondary mathematics assessment and resource database. WWW document [smard.cqu.edu.au]. (accessed 2/01)

This Web site from Australia provides a database of classroom-tested assessment ideas for the secondary classroom. There is also a link to other assessment Web sites provided.

Saskatchewan Education. Templates for assessment and evaluation. WWW document [http://www.sasked.gov.sk.ca/docs/midlmath/tmpmmath.html]. (accessed 2/01).

This page links to PDF files of observation checklists, rating scales, and self-assessment tools that are ready to be printed and used in the classroom.

Schwartz, J. (Director). (1999). Balanced assessment in mathematics. WWW document [gseweb.harvard.edu/~etc/ba/]. (accessed 2/01)

This is the home of the Balanced Assessment project. The site provides information on the project, including personnel, sample assessment tasks, and details about publications.

Science and Mathematics Consortium for Northwest Schools. Assessment resources. WWW document [http://www.col-ed.org/smcnws/assessment.html]. (accessed 2/01).

The site includes a listing of links that have been compiled to help educators analyze assessment issues and design effective assessments.

Texas Education Network. (1999). Resource center: Texas essential knowledge and skills (TEKS). WWW document [http://www.tenet.edu/teks/math/assess/index.html]. (accessed 2/01)

Assessment ideas from the State of Texas are presented, as well as links to many other locations on the Internet that feature assessment activities and ideas.

Wilcox, S., Schoenfeld, A., Burkhardt, H., Ridgeway, J., & Daro, P. (Dirs.). (1999). Balanced assessment project: Example task. WWW document [educ.msu.edu/MARS/tasks]. (accessed 2/01)

This page provides many tasks for assessment projects for grades 4, 8, 10, and 12.

JOURNAL ARTICLES

Asturias, H. (1994). Using students' portfolios to assess mathematical understanding. *Mathematics Teacher*, 87 (9), 698-701.

Asturias, H., Beck, P., & Kerr Stenmark, J. (1994). A room with more than one view. *Mathematics Teaching in the Middle School*, 1 (1), 44-49.

Bernauer, J., & Cress, K. (1997). How school communities can help redefine accountability assessment. *Phi Delta Kappan*, 79 (1), 71-75.

Billstein, R. (1998). The stem model. *Mathematics Teaching in the Middle School*, 3 (4), 282-286, 294-296.

Bishop, E., & Fransen, S. (1998). Building community: An alternative assessment. *Phi Delta Kappan*, 80 (1), 39-40, 57-58.

Black, P., & William D. (1998). Inside the black box: Raising standards through classroom assessment. *Phi Delta Kappan*, 80 (2), 139-148.

Bolte, L. (1999). Using concept maps and interactive essays for assessment in mathematics. *School Science and Mathematics*, 99 (1), 19-25.

Bracey, G. (1994). Standards and assessment. *Phi Delta Kappan*, 76 (2), 166-167.

Brown-Herbst, K. (1999). So math isn't just answers. *Mathematics Teaching in the Middle School*, 4 (7), 448-455.

Cai, J. (2001). Improving mathematics learning: Lessons from cross-national studies of Chinese and U.S. students. *Phi Delta Kappan*, 82 (5), 400-404.

Cai, J., Magone, M., Wang, N., & Lane, S. (1996). Describing student performance qualitatively. *Mathematics Teaching in the Middle School*, 1 (10), 828-835.

Clarke, D. (1995). Quality mathematics: How can we tell? *Mathematics Teacher*, 88 (4), 326-328.

Clarke D., & Wilson, L. (1994). Valuing what we see. *Mathematics Teacher*, 87 (7), 542-545.

Cohen, I., & Fowler, J. (1998). Create assessments that do it all. *Mathematics Teaching in the Middle School*, 4 (1), 44-47.

Cole, K. (1999). Walking around: Getting more from informal assessment. *Mathematics Teaching in the Middle School*, 4 (4), 224-227.

Cole, K., Coffey, J., & Goldman, S. (1999). Using assessments to improve equity in mathematics. *Educational Leadership*, 56 (6), 56-58.

Conway, K. (1999). Assessing open-ended problems. *Mathematics Teaching in the Middle School*, 4 (8), 510-514.

Cooney, T., Bell, K., Fisher-Cauble, D., & Sanchez, W. (1996). The demands of alternative assessment: What teachers say. *Mathematics Teacher*, 89 (6), 484-487.

Crowley, M. (1997). Aligning assessment with classroom practices: A promising testing format. *Mathematics Teacher*, 90 (9), 706-711.

Curcio, F., & Artzt, A. (1996). Assessing students' ability to analyze data: Reaching beyond computation. *Mathematics Teacher*, 89 (8), 668-672.

Darling-Hammond, L., & Falk, B. (1997). Using standards and assessments to support student learning. *Phi Delta Kappan*, 79 (3), 190-199.

Davies, A., & Williams, P. (1997). Accountability. *Phi Delta Kappan*, 79 (1), 76-79.

Driscoll, M. (1995). "The farther out you go...": Assessment in the classroom. *Mathematics Teacher*, 88 (5), 420-425.

Farmer Kearns, J., Kleinert, H., & Kennedy, S. (1999). We need not exclude anyone. *Educational Leadership*, 56 (6), 33-38.

Galindo, E. (1998). Assessing justification and proof in geometry classes taught using dynamic software. *Mathematics Teacher*, 91 (1), 76-82.

Goodrich Andrade, H. (2000). Using rubrics to promote thinking and learning. *Educational Leadership*, 57 (5), 13-18.

Hancock, C. (1995). Enhancing mathematics learning with open-ended questions. *Mathematics Teacher*, 88 (6), 496-499.

Hodgson, T., & Harpster, D. (1997). Looking back in mathematical modeling: Classroom observations and instructional strategies. *School Science and Mathematics*, 97 (5), 260-267.

Kuhs, T. (1994). Portfolio assessment: Making it work for the first time. *Mathematics Teacher*, 87 (5), 332-335.

Lambdin, D. (1995). An open-and-shut case?: Openness in the assessment process. *Mathematics Teacher*, 88 (8), 680-684.

Lavigne, N., & Lajoie, S. (1996). Communicating performance criteria to students through technology. *Mathematics Teacher*, 89 (1), 66-69.

Levinson, C. (2000). Student assessment in eight countries. *Educational Leadership*, 57 (5), 58-61.

Long, C., & Stansbury, K. (1994). Performance assessments for beginning teachers. *Phi Delta Kappan*, 76 (4), 318-322.

Long, V., & Benson, C. (1998). Re: Alignment. *Mathematics Teacher*, 91 (6), 504-508.

Mabry, L. (1999). Writing to the rubric: Lingering effects of traditional standardized testing in direct writing assessment. *Phi Delta Kappan*, 80 (9), 673-679.

Manon, J. (1995). The mathematics test: A new role for an old friend. *Mathematics Teacher*, 88 (2), 138-141.

Mayer, J., & Hillman, S. (1996). Assessing students' thinking through writing. *Mathematics Teacher*, 89 (5), 428-432.

Moskal, B. (2000). An assessment model for the mathematics classroom. *Mathematics Teaching in the Middle School*, 6 (3), 192-194.

Moskal, B. (2000). Understanding student responses to open-ended tasks. *Mathematics Teaching in the Middle School*, 5 (8), 500-505.

Murdock, T. (1999). Discouraging cheating in your classroom. *Mathematics Teacher*, 92 (7), 587-591.

Murphy, T. (1999). Changing assessment practices in an algebra class, or "will this be on the test?" *Mathematics Teacher*, 92 (3), 247-249.

Neill, D. (1997). Transforming student assessment. *Phi Delta Kappan*, 79 (1), 34-40, 58.

Odafe, V. (1998). Students generating test items: A teaching and assessment strategy. *Mathematics Teacher*, 91 (3), 198-202.

Pallrand, G. (1996). The relationship of assessment to knowledge development in science education. *Phi Delta Kappan*, 78 (4), 315-318.

Petit, M., & Zawojewski, J. (1997). Teachers and students learning together about assessing problem solving. *Mathematics Teacher*, 90 (6), 472-477.

Popham, J. (1997). What's wrong — and what's right — with rubrics. *Educational Leadership*, 55 (2), 72-75.

Reys, R., Reys, B., McIntosh, A., Emanuelsson, G., Johansson, B., & Yang, D. (1999). Assessing number sense of students in Australia, Sweden, Taiwan, and the United States. *School Science and Mathematics*, 99 (2), 61-70.

Robinson, D. (1998). Student portfolios in mathematics. *Mathematics Teacher*, 91 (4), 318-325.

Romagnano, L. (2001). The myth of objectivity in mathematics assessment. *Mathematics Teacher*, 94 (1), 31-37.

Santel-Parke, C., & Cai, J. (1997). Does the task truly measure what was intended? *Mathematics Teaching in the Middle School*, 3 (1), 74-82.

Schloemer, C. (1994). An assessment example. *Mathematics Teacher*, 87 (1), 18.

Schloemer, C. (1997). Some practical possibilities for alternative assessment. *Mathematics Teacher*, 90 (1), 46-49.

Shannon, A., & Zawojewski, J. (1995). Mathematics performance assessment: A new game for students. *Mathematics Teacher*, 88 (9), 752-757.

Shaughnessy, M., & Zawojewski, J. (1999). Secondary students' performance on data and chance in the 1996 NAEP. *Mathematics Teacher*, 92 (8), 713-718.

Shimizu, Y., & Lambdin, D. (1997). Assessing students' performance on an extended problem-solving task: A story from a Japanese classroom. *Mathematics Teacher*, 90 (8), 658-664.

Shymansky, J., Chidsey, J., Henriques, L., Enger, S., Yore, L., Wolfe, E., & Jorgensen, M. (1997). Performance assessment in science as a tool to enhance the picture of student learning. *School Science and Mathematics*, 97 (4), 172-183.

Stallings, V., & Tascione, C. (1996). Student self-assessment and self-evaluation. *Mathematics Teacher*, 89 (7), 548-554.

Stiggins, R. (1999). Assessment, student confidence, and school success. *Phi Delta Kappan*, 81 (3), 191-198.

Taylor, K., & Walton, S. (1997). Co-opting standardized tests in the service of learning. *Phi Delta Kappan*, 79 (1), 66-70.

Thompson, D., & Senk, S. (1998). Using rubrics in high school mathematics courses. *Mathematics Teacher*, 91 (9), 786-793.

Tonack, D. (1996). A teacher's views on classroom assessment. *Mathematics Teaching in the Middle School*, 2 (2), 70-73.

Vincent, M., & Wilson, L. (1996). Informal assessment: A story from the classroom. *Mathematics Teacher*, 89 (3), 248-250.

Wilcox, S.K., & Zielinski, R.S. (1997). Using the assessment of students' learning to reshape teaching. *Mathematics Teacher*, 90 (3), 223-229.

Wilcox, S.K. (1998). Another perspective on concept maps: Empowering students. *Mathematics Teaching in the Middle School*, 3 (7), 464-469.

Wineburg, S. (1997). T.S. Elliot, collaboration, and the quandaries of assessment in a rapidly changing world. *Phi Delta Kappan*, 79 (1), 59-65.

Video Materials

Burns, M. (Dir.). (1993). *Mathematics: Assessment understanding: Individual assessments parts 1-3* [Videotape]. White Plains, NY: Cuisenaire Company of America.

Korf, M. (Prod.). (1998). *Mathematics assessment: A video library, K-12: Introduction* [Videotape]. Boston: WGBH Educational Foundation.

Korf, M. (Prod.). (1998). *Mathematics assessment: A video library, K-12: Beyond testing* [Videotape]. Boston: WGBH Educational Foundation.

Korf, M. (Producer). (1998). *Mathematics assessment: A video library, K-12: Middle school assessment* [Videotape]. Boston: WGBH Educational Foundation.

Korf, M. (Prod.). (1998). *Mathematics assessment: A video library, K-12: High school assessment* [Videotape]. Boston: WGBH Educational Foundation.

NOTES

NOTES

NOTES

NOTES

NOTES

NOTES

NOTES